The
CIA
in
Iran

The 1953 Coup and the Origins
Of the US-Iran Divide

AMERICAN FREE PRESS
2006

The CIA in Iran

The 1953 Coup and the Origins Of the US-Iran Divide

ISBN 0-9785733-2-3

First Printing: January 2007

Published by: American Free Press
645 Pennsylvania Ave. SE
Suite 100
Washington, D.C. 20003
1-888-699-NEWS
www.americanfreepress.net

ON THE FRONT COVER:

Deposed Prime Minister Mohammad Mossadeq was led into his court trial only months after a CIA-orchestrated coup overthrew his democratically elected government. The nationalist leader stood accused of treason and trying to undermine Iran's royal family. Set up by U.S. and British agents to appear anti-Islam and pro-communism, Mossadeq fiercely defended himself in court, at one point passing out from exhaustion and the stress of his hearing. Mossadeq was sentenced to death but his sentence was commuted due to his age. He spent the rest of his life under house arrest.

DEDICATION

This book is dedicated to all of the Iranians who lost their lives or suffered as a result of the Anglo-American coup, which in 1953 led to the overthrow of the democratically elected government of Prime Minister Mohammad Mossadeq.

—CJP

ACKNOWLEDGEMENTS

Special thanks for this book go out to John Young of Cryptome.org for his tireless work as a watchdog and truthteller. Also, thanks go to the George Washington University National Security Archive for the wealth of information it provides on its web site and for its efforts to force U.S. government agencies to declassify historic documents such as this report. Finally, thanks go to Iranian and U.S. sources who helped us piece together this important publication.

—CJP

TOP: A DISPIRITED MOHAMMAD MOSSADEQ drops his head to the table during his trial where, ironically, he was accused of committing treason against his own government. In fact, it was Mossadeq who had a reputation for honesty and integrity, strongly opposing foreign meddling in Iran at the time when most Iranians perceived many of their economic and political hardships as originating from such influence. Today, his speeches are still widely read in Iran and his legacy remains untarnished. BOTTOM: Mossadeq strenuously objects to the proceedings.

TABLE OF CONTENTS

MOST AMERICANS HAVE NEVER KNOWN the incredible story of how the Central Intelligence Agency overthrew the government of the democratically elected Iranian Prime Minister Mohammad Mossadeq, shown above while still in office, and replaced him with the repressive and violent Shah. If Americans only knew of this elaborate scheme, which resulted in the execution of many Iranian officials, they would better understand the origins of the Iranian people's justified animosity toward the U.S. government.

PREFACE

IN OCTOBER 2003, WHILE VISITING the dentist's office, I met an Iranian who had recently started there as a dentist. It was just before President George W. Bush had attacked Iraq—a tragic and bloody blunder. The Iranian's name was Ali Fatemi, and we struck up a candid discussion on the Middle East in our brief encounter. At one point in the conversation, I asked Fatemi, somewhat jokingly, if he was related to Hoseyn Fatemi, the maverick nationalist foreign minister under the regime of former Iranian Prime Minister Mohammad Mossadeq. His response surprised me: "He was my uncle," he said.

We then talked about the coup that took place in Iran in 1953, and he told me that his family had fled to San Francisco when it looked as though serious trouble was brewing in his country. He told me that he still remembers the day he found out that his uncle had been killed. He was swimming in the pool of the hotel where his family was staying at the time when they received the news that his uncle Foreign Minister Fatemi had been executed by a firing squad.

I mentioned to him that I had read a redacted version of a secret CIA report detailing how U.S. and British intelligence, from behind the scenes, had planned and orchestrated the coup. Fatemi told me that he had seen the un-redacted version of the report in Farsi, the language of Iran. He knew full-well who was behind the bloody plan to depose Mossadeq and the murder of his uncle.

Since that time, I have related this story to many people to illustrate the anger that Iranians still harbor toward Washington. It is worse than that though, as Iranians' anti-West views have only increased with time. While access to oil dictated Washington's Middle East policy in the 1950s, today, it is the U.S. government's staunch support for Israel, at the expense of the Palestinian people, that has exacerbated the situation.

The simple fact is, for too long Americans have received only half the story of U.S. involvement in Iran, thanks to the craven mainstream U.S. media. Americans fail to understand the context that led to the Iranian Revolution in 1979, which threw out the Shah. And it was this event that led to the hostage crisis, where 50 U.S. embassy staffers in Tehran were held for 444 days by Iranian students, who were reacting to U.S. support for the Shah.

Iranians remember that history well, particularly the days after the CIA successfully carried out its overthrow. Mossadeq stood accused of defying the Shah's order to resign and of trying to overthrow the Iranian regime. He was found guilty and sentenced to death. His sentence was commuted because of his age—he was 70 years old at the time—but he was still forced to serve out the rest of his life in solitary confinement. Others were not so lucky. Thousands of Mossadeq's supporters in government and the military were also rounded up in the days following the coup, and hundreds of them were executed just like Fatemi's uncle.

As the United States and Iran are now again in confrontation, it is critical that we look back to 1953, when U.S. intelligence, working in conjunction with the British, bought off key officials in the Iranian government and the military, committed acts of terrorism and set up a once popular Iranian prime minister for the purpose of overthrowing a secular populist government that had been taking root there. And that is why *American Free Press* is publishing this once top-secret CIA document, which provides the often shocking details of how secret intelligence operatives, working out of the U.S. embassy, planned the overthrow of the democratically elected government of Iran, led by Mossadeq. For America to understand the deep-seated anti-West views held by many Iranians today, we must go back to 1953.

It is with this in mind that *American Free Press* is bringing you the full report, published in the United States for the first time with only minimal redactions. There are other versions of this report in circulation, but no other national media outlet has worked with sources that include a member of Mossadeq's one-time party, the National Front, to fill in the missing pieces and correct erroneous information.

Historians today speculate on what Iran would look like in the twenty-first century had it not been for U.S. and British meddling that brought about this bloody overthrow. Would it still be the Islamic republic that it is now? An interesting question to stew on.

In any event, we can at least agree on one thing: there was no way to know what would happen once the ball was set in motion. The coup in Iran highlights the many reasons why government men, in all their arrogance, should not seek to change history by such sinister means. It is a classic case of "you reap what you sow."

That is why it is imperative that we learn the truth about what happened in our history so we can be better informed and make better decisions today. And that is the purpose of releasing this book some 50 years after the tragic event. May we learn from our past, so we can better understand our present.

Christopher J. Petherick
Editor, *American Free Press*

[Clandestine Service]
Historical Paper No. 208

CLANDESTINE SERVICE HISTORY

OVERTHROW OF
PREMIER MOSSADEQ
OF IRAN
November 1952-August 1953

Date written: March 1954
Date published: October 1969
Written by: Dr. Donald N. Wilber

HISTORIAN'S NOTE

THIS STUDY WAS ORIGINALLY ENTITLED *Overthrow of Premier Mossadeq of Iran* and was written in March 1954 by Dr. Donald N. Wilber, who had played an active role in the operation. The study was written because it seemed desirable to have a record of a major operation prepared while documents were readily at hand and while the memories of the personnel involved in the activity were still fresh. In addition, it was felt advisable to stress certain conclusions reached after the operation had been completed and to embody some of these in the form of recommendations applicable to future, parallel operations. Documents pertaining to the operation described in this paper are in the Project Ajax files which are held by the Iran Branch of the Near East and South Asia Division. All names mentioned in this paper have been checked for accuracy and completeness. A serious effort has been made to supply the first name and middle initial of each individual. The omission of any first names and middle initials indicates that such information could not be located.

Dean L. Dodge
State Department
Near East Division
Historical Officer
March 1969

IN 1953, UNDERSECRETARY OF STATE General Walter Bedell "Beetle" Smith, fresh off his post as director of the CIA, was one of the driving forces behind the U.S. operation to depose Prime Minister Mossadeq and eliminate the nationalists from the Iranian government. It was Smith's directive that resulted in a policy shift for the CIA and started the ball rolling to stage a coup d'etat in Iran.

1

PRELIMINARY STEPS

REPRESENTATIVES OF BRITISH INTELLIGENCE met with Near East and Africa (NEA) Division representatives in Washington during November and December 1952 for the purpose of discussing joint war and stay behind plans in Iran. In attendance for British Intelligence were Mr. Christopher Montague Woodhouse, recently Chief of Station for British Intelligence in Tehran; Mr. Samuel Falle of the British Intelligence Station in Tehran; and Mr. John Bruce Lockhart, SIS Washington representative. In attendance for NEA Division were Mr. Kermit Roosevelt, Chief of Division, Mr. John H. Leavitt, Chief of Iran Branch; Mr. John W. Pendleton, Deputy Chief of Division; and Mr. James A. Darling, Chief of NEA Paramilitary Staff.

Although it was not on the previously agreed agenda of the meeting, British Intelligence representatives brought up the proposition of a joint political action to remove Prime Minister Mossadeq. The NEA Division had not intended to discuss this question at all and was unprepared to do so.

The meeting concluded without any decision being made and with the NEA Division committing itself only to study in more detail the political action proposals advanced by British Intelligence.

In March 1953 a telegram was received from the Tehran Station which stated that General [REDACTED] had contacted the assistant military attache and had requested Ambassador [Loy] Henderson's views as to whether or nor the U.S. Government was interested in covertly supporting an Iranian military effort to oust Premier Mossadeq. A meeting was held in the Embassy at which Headquarters personnel, then in the field, and station personnel were in attendance. A cautiously worded reply was drafted at Headquarters and its substance delivered to General [REDACTED]. The reply did not commit the United States in any way but was mildly encouraging and revealed some U.S. interest in the idea. On the basis of the [REDACTED] overture and other clear signs that determined opposition to Mossadeq was taking shape, and in view of the totally destructive and reckless attitude of the government of Prime Minister Mossadeq, General Walter Bedell Smith, Undersecretary of State, determined that the U.S. government could no longer approve of the Mossadeq government and would prefer a successor government in which there would be no National Frontists. The change in policy was communicated to CIA, and the NEA Division was informed that it was authorized to consider operations which would contribute to the fall of the Mossadeq government. The Department of State and CIA jointly informed Ambassador Henderson and the Chief of Station, Roger Goiran, of the new policy and of the operational authorization. The Director, on 4 April 1953, approved a budget of $1,000,000 which could be used by the Tehran Station in any way that would bring about the fall of Mossadeq. Full authority was given to Ambassador Henderson and the Chief of Station enabling any part or all of the $1,000,000 to be used without further authority, as long as the Ambassador and the station concurred. On 16 April 1953 a comprehensive study entitled: "Factors Involved in the Overthrow of Mossadeq" was completed. The study indicated that a Shah-General Zahedi combination, supported by CIA local assets and financial backing, would have a good chance of overthrowing Mossadeq, particularly if this combination should be able to get the largest mobs in the streets and if a sizable portion of the Tehran garrison refused to carry out Mossadeq's orders.

Subsequent contact was made with General [REDACTED]. Although his motives appeared serious, it soon became apparent that he had no concrete plan and was in fact in no position to take action against Mossadeq. General Zahedi, who at one time was a member of Mossadeq's cabinet, stood out as the only major personality in undisguised opposition to Mossadeq. For this reason he attached to himself a considerable following. The Tehran Station, in April 1953, reestablished covert contact with Zahedi through Commander Eric Pollard, the U.S. Naval Attache. In order to make the covert liaison with Zahedi more effective and reliable, and also for security reasons, Zahedi's son, Ardeshir Zahedi, was selected as the means of contact with General Zahedi in June 1953. After 21 July 1953, contact with General Zahedi was made directly.

THE ABOVE PHOTOGRAPH SHOWS CIA OPERATIVE Dr. Donald Wilber
while he was in Egypt in 1930. Wilber was the one of the principal organizers
of Operation Ajax, the coup to overthrow the democratically elected government of Iranian Prime Minister Mohammad Mossadeq. While serving in the
Middle East as a covert operative for U.S. intelligence, Wilber, a specialist on
Iran and Afghanistan, wrote extensively about his travels and was also
renowned as an expert on oriental rugs.

2

DRAFTING THE PLAN

NEAR THE END OF APRIL 1953 Dr. Donald N. Wilber, covert consultant to NEA, was selected by the Division to go to Nicosia and, in close collaboration with SIS, draw up a plan for the overthrow of Mossadeq. The assumption by Headquarters was that the planners would come up with a project which they could conscientiously recommend. The discussions were begun at Nicosia on 13 May 1953 between Wilber and SIS Officer Norman Matthew Darbyshire. Occasionally Mr. H. John Collins, Chief of SIS station at Nicosia, was also present. Mr. Darbyshire, who was in charge of SIS's Iran branch, had been in Iran for several years and was fluent in the language. Discussions were concluded on 30 May 1953, and the completed draft of a recommended operational plan was cabled by Dr. Wilber to Headquarters on 1 June.

The opening meeting consisted of a review of all the important personalities on the political scene in Iran with a view toward determining whether General Zahedi, the most prominent politician in opposition to Mossadeq, was in fact the sole figure worthy of support and, if so, what individuals and elements should be enlisted in his support. It soon became apparent that Dr. Wilber and Mr. Darbyshire held quite similar views of Iranian personalities and had made very similar estimates of the factors involved in the Iranian political scene. There was no friction or marked difference of opinion during the discussions. It also quickly became apparent that the SIS was perfectly content to follow whatever lead was taken by the Agency. It seemed obvious to Wilber that the British were very pleased at having obtained the active cooperation of the Agency and were determined to do nothing which might jeopardize U.S. participation. At the same time there was a faint note of envy expressed over the fact that the Agency was better equipped in the way of funds, personnel, and facilities than was SIS. Wilber reported the preliminary conversations concerning a three-way channel, set up for this occasion, which was designed to ensure immediate relay between Washington, Nicosia, and Tehran. That is, a message originating at any one of these places would be sent by the most expeditious route to the other two. This route was the Middle East Communications Authority (MECA) link, the relay station a few miles outside of Nicosia.*

Discussions at Nicosia moved on to a disclosure of assets by both parties. Those by SIS were centered upon the contacts of the Rashidian brothers in such fields as the armed forces, the Majlis (Iranian Parliament), religious leaders, the press, street gangs, politicians, and other influential figures. When this material was relayed from Nicosia, the Tehran Station commented that it was their belief that these assets had been far overstated and oversold. In reply it was pointed out that SIS was as aware as we of the weaknesses of the Rashidians, but that one of the strongest points in their favor was their avowed willingness to risk their possessions and their lives in an attempt against Mossadeq. In the critical days of August 1953 [the Rashidian brothers**] did display such a willingness. SIS disclosures were followed by those of Dr. Wilber for CIA. Prior to Wilber's departure a discussion was held at Headquarters to determine which of the station assets should be disclosed to the SIS in return for promised disclosures by the SIS

---

* Unfortunately, communications between Nicosia and Tehran were not as rapid as was hoped during this period in which more than 45 cables were exchanged.

** Please see page 49 for a brief bio of the Rashidian brothers, who were instrumental in assisting the CIA and Britain's SIS in carrying out the coup.

of the assets which they were prepared to put into an operational plan. It was agreed at Headquarters that the identities of the vitally important principal agents of the Tehran Station, [Jalili] [and Kayvani] [REDACTED] would not be disclosed. Since the SIS had been informed during the November 1952 meetings referred to above that CIA had two major principal agents in Iran, it was necessary to offer two such in place of [Jalili and] [Kayvani]. This was done, naming a station agent and a sub-agent of [REDACTED] to these important posts. To the best of our knowledge [Jalili and Kayvani] were not uncovered by the Rashidian brothers or any other SIS agents during the course of this operation.

The continuing conversations at Nicosia were reflected by outgoing cables requesting, principally from the Tehran Station, information which would be helpful in drafting the operational plan.

Discussions now narrowed down to a series of basic assumptions which were stressed both in the draft plan and in its final form. It was determined that the details of the operational plan should be included within a framework of such basic assumptions as these: that Zahedi alone of potential candidates had the vigor and courage to make him worthy of support; that the Shah must be brought into the operation; that the Shah would act only with great reluctance but that he could be forced to do so; that if the issue was clear-cut the armed forces would follow the Shah rather than Mossadeq; that the operation must, if possible, be made to appear legal or quasi-legal instead of an outright coup; that public opinion must be fanned to fever pitch against Mossadeq in the period just preceding the execution of the overthrow operation; that the military aspect would be successful only if the station were able to review the plan with the Iranians chosen by Zahedi to execute it; that immediate precautions must be taken by the new government to meet a strong reaction by the [communist] Tudeh Party. Some of these assumptions were presented in cables sent off before the draft plan was completed. The reactions from the Tehran Station and Headquarters did not always express agreement with the ideas of the planners. The station expressed its feeling that the Shah would not act decisively against Mossadeq, while Headquarters wondered whether we should not support some other individual and whether the Persians themselves might not take the lead in action designed to overthrow Mossadeq. It was, however, agreed that the station should begin at once with its new policy of attacking the government of Mossadeq through gray propaganda.* The station relayed this line to its own agents and passed it on to the Rashidian brothers of SIS. The CIA Art Group was asked to prepare a considerable number of anti-Mossadeq cartoons. The meetings were interrupted for several days when one of the Rashidian brothers managed to get permission to leave Iran**—not at all an easy matter during the Mossadeq period— and went to Geneva where he was met by SIS Officer Norman Darbyshire. He not only briefed Darbyshire on the current situation but was able to give comprehensive answers to a number of specific questions. It should be noted that the SIS station at Nicosia had been in tri-weekly wireless contact with the Rashidian brothers at Tehran, employing the best of the British trained stay behind operators. This contact, in Persian, was naturally limited in time, and even more limited after we passed word to Darbyshire on his return from Geneva that the Iranian armed forces were now in possession of [radio] directional finders. Mr. George A. Carroll (Foreign Intelligence Deputy Tehran, Designate) arrived at Nicosia on 29 May, in time to pass along reactions and suggestions from Headquarters, prior to the completion of the draft plan. As stated, this draft was cabled to Headquarters on 1 June 1953. (See Appendix A for a typed transcript of the cable.) While Nicosia

---

* "Gray propaganda" refers to propaganda put out without any clear indication as to its source. This is in contrast to "black propaganda," which is attributed to a source in an effort to discredit it or implicate it.

** It is interesting to note that Rashidian obtained his exit visa to leave Iran and his reentry permit from no less a supporter of Mossadeq than Foreign Minister Hoseyn Fatemi. This lends some evidence to long held CIA views that Fatemi was from time to time susceptible to British overtures and was trying to keep a hand in with the opposition and British in the event Mossadeq fell. He was certainly aware of Rashidian's agent status with the British.

proved to be a handy point of contact with the British and a fairly good communications intersection point, it did have certain disadvantages. It was remote from the headquarters of either agency, and, even worse, the SIS station files were extremely inadequate so that any information on personalities, especially members of the Iranian armed forces, had to be obtained by querying the Tehran Station and Headquarters.

Once the draft plan had been cabled, it was agreed with SIS that their copy would be hand-carried to London where the viewpoint of the SIS headquarters would be incorporated prior to 15 June. In the meantime, as had been agreed with Headquarters, the Agency would conduct a searching scrutiny of the plan at Beirut, and then bring these results to London for amalgamation with the draft as reworked by SIS at London. Carroll remained a few days after the completion of the draft to begin work on the military aspect of the plan. He also returned to Nicosia for a few additional days after the close of the Beirut meetings for this purpose. It must be noted that Miss Helen E. Morgan, CIA representative at Nicosia, gave strong support to the CIA personnel who worked at Nicosia.

KERMIT ROOSEVELT was the head of the CIA's Near East Division in 1953. Roosevelt, the grandson of former U.S. President Theodore Roosevelt, was tasked by Secretary of State John Foster Dulles and CIA Director Allen Dulles with carrying out the plan to depose Mossadeq and replace him with the Shah. In his 1979 book on the operation, Roosevelt wrote that, upon taking power, the Shah said: "'I owe my throne to God, my people, my army and to you!' By 'you' [the Shah] meant me and the two countries—Great Britain and the United Sates—I was representing. We were all heroes."

3

THE OPERATIONAL PLAN

ON THE AFTERNOON OF 9 JUNE all those who were to take part in the discussions arrived in Beirut: Mr. Kermit Roosevelt, Chief NEA and project chief throughout the operation, came in by plane from London; Carroll came from Cyprus by plane; Roger Goiran, Chief of Station at Tehran, drove in from Damascus by car; and Wilber came in from Cairo by air.

On the morning of 10 June the talks got under way and continued for four days. The usual schedule was to start quite early, carry through until about two o'clock, and then assemble again in the late afternoon. The first order of business was a reexamination of all the factors and elements of the political scene in Iran in light of the current and comprehensive information supplied by the Tehran chief of station. After all the basic principles of the draft plan had been accepted, the attention of the conferees turned to a section by section consideration of the plan. The object of the meetings was to determine how each section could be given the maximum structure and impact. One switch in general outlook was made that was most salutary for all later thinking. The draft plan had implied that definite counteraction would have to be taken against some of the strongest elements supporting Mossadeq, such as the Qashqai tribal leaders; but it was now decided that every effort should be devoted to increasing the size and effectiveness of the anti-Mossadeq forces, the assumption being that Mossadeq's supporting elements would not react once their leader was out of the picture.

The Tehran chief of station suggested that an alternative plan to provide for the overthrow of Mossadeq be developed. This was to become the Amini/Qashqai plan which the station kept alive as a possible alternative until the successful conclusion of Ajax. Saturday afternoon the group held its final meeting and on the next morning, 14 June, departed by plane for its several destinations.

Roosevelt and Wilber arrived in London on 15 June and reported to the main offices of the SIS at 54 Broadway. They turned over the Beirut revision of the plan. No copy of the original Beirut draft exists, since it was reworked to form the final "London" draft.

The London meetings were held in one of the conference rooms at 54 Broadway, notable only for a large sign with the legend in red, "Curb Your Guests." For the SIS, Commander Maurice M. Firth and Norman Darbyshire, who had come on from Nicosia by way of Geneva (where he had seen Asadollah Rashidian a second time before the latter went back to Iran) were always present. Upon occasion Major P. (Paddy) J. Keen, whose post seemed to be that of desk officer for several Middle East countries, also participated. Montague Woodhouse, clearly one of their most highly esteemed officers, attended a single meeting but had little to contribute.

From the moment the discussion began, it was clear that the SIS had no major comments of their own on the draft plan. Nor did they have much to say on the Beirut version beyond a certain close attention to phraseology. As at Nicosia it was apparent that the Americans were to be placated and allowed to run things as they pleased. They did, however, seem to have abundant confidence in the plan and in the successful outcome of the operation, and said that the Rashidians would be ordered to follow completely the orders of CIA's Tehran Station.

At the final meeting those present reviewed the future conduct of affairs. The SIS officers stated that they thought it would take some time to obtain a firm decision from their government as to the approval or non-approval of the plan.

Roosevelt and Wilber left London on 17 June, and Roosevelt was back in his office by noon of the 18th.

There the plan was immediately reconstructed and typed up. It is given as Appendix B.

IN 1953, SECRETARY OF STATE John Foster Dulles, shown here with President Eisenhower in 1956, was named *Time* magazine's "Man of the Year" for his efforts to fight the spread of communism. U.S. officials, such as Dulles, exploited the threat of communism and the spread of Soviet influence to justify orchestrating a coup in Iran in that year. Objective historians now contend that it was Mossadeq's call to nationalize Iran's oil, which left out the British Anglo-Iranian Oil Company, that actually prompted the elaborate scheme.

4

ACTIVITY BEGINS

SINCE THE MEETINGS AT BEIRUT AND LONDON had taken such a relatively short time, there was not too much that Headquarters could do in the interval from the time of Roosevelt's departure until his return. Progress had, however, been made in setting up a specific and close liaison with the State Department. The fact that an operational plan was being prepared was already known to a very restricted number of individuals in the State Department, and it should be noted that the security there seems to have been excellent up to the time of the event.

[Those individuals include: Secretary of State John Foster Dulles; Under Secretary of State General Walter Bedell Smith; Deputy Under Secretary of State Harrison Freeman Matthews; Assistant Secretary of State/NEA, Mr. Henry A. Byroade; Deputy Assistant Secretary of State/NEA, Mr. John Durnford Jernagan; and Liaison, Mr. James Lampton Berry.]

The Greece-Turkey-Iran (GTI) Office of the Department of State presented its informed opinion in two papers: one was a top secret paper of 6 June 1953 entitled, "Proposal to Bring about a Change of Government in Iran" and the other a top secret undated GTI memorandum on the subject, "Measures which the United States Government might take in support of a successor government to Mossadeq."*

It was not the task of officers of the State Department to obtain high level decisions on the plan. However, the State Department did assert that, prior to acceptance of the plan, assurance must be forthcoming from the British that they would be flexible in their approach to the government that succeeded Mossadeq as far as the oil question was concerned.

Mr. Leslie Herbert Mitchell, UK Embassy officer (SIS representative) charged with liaison with the Agency, concerned himself with this point and did expedite the required assurances from the British Government. These assurances took the form of a foreign office memorandum presented by British Ambassador to the United States, Roger Mellor Makins, to Under Secretary of State Smith on 23 July 1953. (Copy attached as Appendix C.) Also the Department of State wanted to satisfy itself that an adequate amount of interim economic aid would be forthcoming to the successor government before it would finally approve decisive action.

During this same period discussions between Agency officers and Ambassador Henderson (in Washington, having arrived on consultation 3 June) began 8 June. (This is recorded in a memorandum of conversation contained in Ajax files.) The Ambassador appeared to backtrack somewhat from his earlier opinion that the premise of the plan that the Shah would cooperate was fallacious, and that the Shah would not issue a *farman* naming Zahedi unless in response to a vote of inclination by the Majlis. The Ambassador, who was always thoroughly cooperative, was absorbed in a search for constructive suggestions and willingly agreed to delay his return to Tehran by arranging a prolonged visit in Europe. From the standpoint of the plan it was not considered advisable to have the Ambassador in Tehran when the final operation was undertaken. In addition, his continued absence was thought to be an

---

* A precursor to Operation Ajax, which was the plan set forth by Kermit Roosevelt and Donald Wilber, was named "Operation Be Damned." This was a plan created by U.S. intelligence on how to carry out the overthrow of the Iranian government.

important factor in the war of nerves which was to be conducted against Mossadeq.

The following approvals of the operational plan were obtained on the dates indicated:

> Director SIS: 1 July 1953
> Foreign Secretary: 1 July 1953
> Prime Minister: 1 July 1953
> Secretary of State: 11 July 1953
> Director CIA: 11 July 1953
> President: 11 July 1953

Pending final approval or disapproval of the operational plan, the station was carrying forward activities already authorized toward the achievement of the goal.

In addition to the general authorization of April enabling the Tehran Station to spend up to $1,000,000 in covert activity in support of Zahedi, the station on 20 May was specifically authorized to spend one million rials a week (rate of 90 rials to the U.S. dollar) in purchasing the cooperation of members of the Iranian Majlis. On or about the end of June the station had established direct contact with the Rashidian brothers and was prepared to instruct them as to their role and those of their contacts in the development of the operation.

At Headquarters two groups were organized within the NE/4 Branch on 22 June in support of Tehran Station operational preparations. One group, headed by Carroll who had returned from Nicosia in mid-June, was to make an exhaustive study of the military aspects of the overthrow operation.

Carroll's final report on the military aspect of Ajax planning is attached as Appendix D.

The intent was to present Zahedi and his chosen military secretariat with a concrete plan for their modification or improvement. It was felt that every effort should be made to bring the rather long-winded and often illogical Persians into a position where each one knew exactly what specific action was required of him. The soundness of this feeling was demonstrated when the failure of the Persians to maintain security resulted in the initial breakdown. The other group, headed by Wilber, assumed responsibility for the psychological warfare phases of the plan. Overall direction of these groups and of relations with the field station were in the hands of Mr. John Henry Waller, head of NE/4 Branch.

Carroll left for Tehran in mid-July. He stopped over at London to discuss his military plan with SIS Officer Norman Darbyshire and finally reached Tehran on 21 July.

Wilber's group sent guidance cables and dispatches to the station, all intended to flesh up the skeleton of psychological operations as presented in the plan itself. In the meantime a considerable number of anti-Mossadeq articles were written or outlined by the group while the CIA Art Group was given constant guidance in its preparation of a large number of anti-Mossadeq cartoons and broadsheets. In addition, these artists did an effective drawing for a wall poster showing Zahedi being presented to the Iranian people by the Shah. Written and illustrative material piled up rapidly, and on 19 July a special courier took it all to Tehran. On 22 July the station began to distribute the material to several agents. What happened to this material will be described in later pages.

By the time that the go-ahead had been received from all parties involved, the NEA Division had picked out qualified individuals for special assignments connected with the project: Mr. Roosevelt, Chief, NEA, was to be field commander in Tehran; John H. Leavitt, NEA/CPP, was to go to Nicosia to be in contact and liaison with the SIS station and to maintain the three-way wireless contact established earlier; while Colonel Stephen Johnson Meads drew the job of representing the Agency in meetings in Paris with Princess Ashraf, energetic twin sister of the Shah. Mr. Joseph C. Goodwin, Chief of Station in Tehran, was to act for purposes of Ajax as chief of staff to the field commander, Mr. Roosevelt. Mr. George Carroll, Chief FI Tehran, was given the military planning responsibility first in Washington, then in Tehran. Dr. Donald Wilber was charged throughout the operation with the propaganda aspects of the plan and worked closely with the CIA Art Group in the preparation of propaganda material. Mr. John Waller, just having returned from service as Chief FI, Tehran, was charged with the Headquarters support responsibilities during Ajax and maintained the required liaison with the Departments of State and Defense. Although not present in Tehran for the final implementation of Ajax, Mr. Roger Goiran, previous Chief of Station Tehran, directed the early stages and preliminaries of the operation in Tehran. It should be here noted that Mr. Goiran, more than any other officer, was responsible for having developed, over a five-year period, station assets which proved valuable and necessary to the operation.

THIS PHOTOGRAPH WAS TAKEN OF THE SHAH and his wife, Soraya Esfandiary, as they came off an airplane at the airport in Rome in 1953. (The man in the center is unidentified.) The Shah was arriving in Italy at a time when it appeared the coup had failed. Much to the dismay of CIA and SIS agents, who were working inside Iran to carry out the operation, the Shah reportedly issued statements from a safe distance to the press that did not incite a violent street response.

5

MOUNTING PRESSURE
AGAINST THE SHAH

FROM THE VERY BEGINNING it had been recognized that the Shah must be forced to play a specific role, however reluctant he might prove to be. Therefore, the plan presented a series of measures designed to rid him once and for all of his pathological fear of the "hidden hand" of the British, and to assure him that the United States and the United Kingdom would firmly support him and had both resolved that Mossadeq must go. The measures were also intended to produce such pressure on the Shah that it would be easier for him to sign the papers required of him than it would be to refuse.

On 23 June the timetable covering all the envoys to be sent to the Shah was drawn up at Headquarters. In execution all these steps went off as planned.

The initial task was to brief Princess Ashraf, who was thought to be in Paris at that time. It was planned to approach her about 10 July in Paris and have her back in Tehran to see the Shah about 20 July. Asodollah Rashidian, still in Geneva, was to call upon her first and prepare her for the joint visit of Darbyshire for SIS and Meade for CIA. (SIS had assured Headquarters that this call could be made in Paris at any time.) Meade arrived in London by air on

10 July and went at once to Paris with Darbyshire. Then an unanticipated delay occurred. Princess Ashraf was not in Paris, and it was not until the 15th that she was located on the Riviera and visited by Asodollah Rashidian.

He reported that she had shown no enthusiasm at all with regard to her proposed role. However, the next day the "official" representatives had two meetings with her and she agreed to do everything that was asked of her. She did say that her arrival would arouse a strong reaction from the pro-Mossadeq press and hoped that we would be able to put out effective counterblasts. Meade reported in London to Roosevelt and Leavitt. He then returned to Paris and stayed close to Ashraf until her departure for Iran.

Ashraf reached Tehran as a passenger on a commercial flight on 25 July. As expected, her unauthorized return did create a real storm. Neither the Shah, himself, nor the government of Mossadeq had been asked to permit her to return. Both were furious. The Shah refused to see her but did accept a letter passed on through the medium of [Soleiman Behbudi], head of the Shah's household, who was loyal and devoted in an effective way throughout this period. This letter contained news that U.S. General [Herbert Norman] Schwarzkopf [the father of General H. Norman Schwarzkopf of Iraq War I] was coming to see the Shah on an errand similar to that of Ashraf, herself. The Shah welcomed this news and received his sister on the evening of 29 July. The session opened stormily but ended on a note of reconciliation. On the next day she took a plane back to Europe. This was as had been planned, but it came as a relief to know that she was out of the country in view of the pro-Mossadeq press reaction.

The second emissary arrived on the scene in the person of Asadollah Rashidian, the principal SIS agent. According to the plan, Asadollah Rashidian's initial task with the Shah was to convince the ruler that Rashidian was the official spokesman of the UK Government. The advance plan, that of having the Shah select a key phrase which would then be broadcast on the British Broadcasting Company (BBC) Persian language program on certain dates, was followed.

In London the necessary arrangements had been made by Darbyshire to send the phrase over the BBC. On 30 July and again on the 31st the Shah saw Asadollah Rashidian. He had heard the broadcast, but he requested time to assess the situation. Asadollah was, however, able to prepare the Shah for the visit of the American emissary, General Schwarzkopf, and to stress the point that this emissary would repeat the message and, hence, give an additional guarantee of the close collaboration between the United Kingdom and the United States in this undertaking. Schwarzkopf had been chosen by the drafters of the operational plan because of the fact that he had enjoyed the friendship and respect of the Shah in the period from 1942 until 1948 when he headed the U.S. Military Mission to the Iranian Gendarmerie. Approached on 26 June 1953 by John Waller, Chief of NE/4, and briefed at Headquarters on 19 July, Schwarzkopf took to his mission with relish. He said that he had a reputation with the Shah for telling him unpleasant truths that others withheld from him, and he stated that he was sure he could get the required cooperation from the Shah. Schwarzkopf was given a cover mission consisting of a short tour to Lebanon, Pakistan, and Egypt so that his visit to Tehran would appear as a brief stop en route to a principal destination. Schwarzkopf left by air for Beirut on 21 July.

Schwarzkopf's mission was to obtain from the Shah the three papers which are described more fully in the operational plan. They were: (1) a *farman* naming Zahedi as Chief of Staff, (2) a letter indicating his faith in Zahedi which the latter could employ to recruit army officers for the plan in the name of the Shah, and (3) a *farman* calling on all ranks of the army to support his legal Chief of Staff. It was felt that it would be easier to get the Shah to sign such statements than to issue a *farman* dismissing Mossadeq. It was also believed that the action of replacing Mossadeq would be initiated through the Majlis.

Certain events of 21 July at Tehran both shocked and aroused from their attitude of complacency the more conservative elements which had firmly supported Mossadeq.

Demonstrations marked the anniversary of rioting against the government of [previous prime minister] Qavam and of efforts made at that time, two years earlier, to settle the oil issue. However, it was obvious to all that the number of Tudeh participants far outnumbered those assembled by the National Front, and it was this fact more than anything else which alerted the thinking public to the strength acquired by the Tudeh under the Mossadeq government. At this time station personnel were active on several fronts. The propaganda campaign against Mossadeq was now gaining momentum. [REDACTED] owner of [REDACTED] was granted a personal loan of some $45,000 on signed notes in the belief that this would make his organ amenable to our purposes. Headquarters-prepared propaganda material was turned over by the station to Asadollah Rashidian, and by the end of the month an entirely separate and especially planned campaign in favor of the Shah as opposed to Mossadeq was under way in Azerbaijan. The parallel and alternative plan of keeping in close touch with the [REDACTED] combination for the purposes of diverting their attention from Ajax and of discovering the plans and strength of this group remained in effect. Talks with the [REDACTED] continued. At one point the station suggested sending one of the brothers to this country, and Headquarters made an immediate investigation of the mechanics required for making such a trip. The SIS was informed of these talks, and they suggested that their facilities might be used to stir up tribal revolts in the homeland of the [REDACTED].

The station was now in direct contact with Zahedi, who had left his sanctuary in the Majlis on 21 July. After several meetings Station Chief Goiran and Station Chief Designate Goodwin reported that Zahedi appeared lacking in drive, energy, and concrete plans. They concluded that he must be closely guided and that the necessary plans must be made for him.

By 26 July a number of key individuals had moved into position: Roosevelt and Schwarzkopf were at Tehran, Leavitt had been at Nicosia for several days, and Ambassador Henderson had come to rest at Salzburg, where he was to remain, anxious but cooperative, for the next two weeks. At Nicosia, Leavitt did a most capable job of reassuring SIS officials who frequently felt that they were not receiving enough current information. Concomitantly, these SIS officials passed on valuable suggestions coming from London, such as detailed plans for putting the central telephone exchange out of operation.

With Roosevelt's arrival in Tehran the situation was restudied. As a part of the war of nerves against Mossadeq, it was considered advisable to cut down close contacts between high-ranking U.S. officials and officials of Mossadeq's government. Technical Cooperation in Iran (TCI) Director William E. Warne was requested to reduce his normal government contacts, and General Frank McClure, Chief of the U.S. Military Mission in Iran, was requested to appear less friendly with those general officers who were firmly supporting Mossadeq. At this stage it was decided to alter the nature and number of documents which would have to be signed by the Shah. These documents would be limited to one *farman* naming Zahedi as Chief of Staff and one letter denouncing the government-staged referendum on the question of the dissolution of the Majlis as an illegal proceeding. As the month of July ended, station personnel in charge of the propaganda campaign reported on the effective anti-[REDACTED]. It was stated that very effective use had been made of the 28 July statement by Secretary of State Dulles* (made at CIA's suggestion). A request was made that U.S. papers reflect the Iranian press campaign against Mossadeq and that inspired articles be placed in the U.S. press.

On 1 August, two days after Princess Ashraf had left Iran and the Shah had heard the BBC message designed to convince him that Asadollah Rashidian was the official spokesman of the UK Government, Schwarzkopf had an extended meeting with the Shah. Fearful of planted microphones, the Shah led the General into a grand ballroom, pulled a small table to its exact center, and

---

* This statement, made at a press conference, was as follows: "The growing activities of the illegal Communist Party in Iran and the toleration of them by the Iranian Government [have] caused our government concern. These developments make it more difficult to grant aid to Iran."

then both sat on the table. The Shah rejected the proposal that he sign the required documents at once, asserting that he was not fully confident of the loyalty of the army; that he must give advance approval for all members of a new cabinet; and that he must have time to make his own estimate as to the probable success or failure of the undertaking. On the other hand, he said that should Mossadeq carry through his referendum and dissolve the Majlis then he, himself, would have full powers under the constitution to dismiss Mossadeq and replace him with a prime minister of his own choice. This meeting was to be followed by a series of additional ones, some between Roosevelt and the Shah and some between Rashidian and the Shah, in which relentless pressure was exerted in frustrating attempts to overcome an entrenched attitude of vacillation and indecision. On 2 August Roger Goiran, for so long the experienced and valuable chief of station, left Tehran headed for Headquarters duty. While his knowledge had been of inestimable value in the preparatory stages of Ajax, it was judged that his departure at just this time would be an important factor in the war of nerves against Mossadeq, and in the planned efforts to confuse and disturb the potential opposition. By this time the Counselor, Gordon Henry Mattison, and the ranking political officer, Mr. Roy Malcolm Melbourne, had been briefed on Ajax and were discreetly helpful. Mattison, in interviews with [REDACTED], followed station direction in a successful effort to divert attention of the [REDACTED] group from the real purpose of Ajax.

During this period Mossadeq, as always, had been on the alert to try to hold the initiative and keep his growing opposition off balance. His attention turned toward the Majlis, where opposition appeared to be hardening. On 14 July he directed the deputies supporting the government to resign. Several of the neutral or timidly anti-Mossadeq deputies followed suit until a total of 28 had resigned. Headquarters urged that the anti-Mossadeq deputies be given every encouragement to keep their posts and to take up *bast* (political sanctuary) in the Majlis. The theme to be built up was that those who had not resigned from the Majlis would constitute the legitimate parliamentary body. This stand was at least partially responsible for Mossadeq's growing belief that the body must be dissolved. Such action would leave him as the undisputed dictator of the country since his full-powers bill had several months more to run. However, he still had to get around the provision of the [Iranian] constitution that only the Shah had the authority to dissolve the Majlis. He did this by staging a national referendum in which the people were to state "yes" or "no" to the question as to whether the Majlis should be dissolved. The referendum was a clear and palpable fake. Held throughout the country beginning 4 August, some two million were said to have voted for dissolution and only a few hundred against. As a maneuver the action was not as satisfactory as Mossadeq anticipated since it clearly revealed abuse of the constitution. This provided an issue on which Mossadeq could be relentlessly attacked by the CIA/SIS subsidized opposition press. The action also did much to alarm the more stable and established elements of the populace, who were nationalists along with everyone else, but who did not favor such a fraudulent breach of the constitution.

During the days of the referendum the station reported in detail on the multiple efforts of station agents to exploit the illegality of this referendum, both before and during the event. Also every declaration made by a religious leader in these days stressed this point. The station indicated that some 20 local newspapers were now in violent opposition to Mossadeq and that some 15 Headquarters-prepared anti-Mossadeq cartoons had appeared in these papers during the referendum week. On 4 August word reached the station that Mossadeq was aware of the true purpose of the visit of Ashraf, and the personnel on the scene felt strongly that action must be mounted very soon. On 4 August Ambassador Henderson, per schedule, set out from Salzburg for Tehran. He was to be met on 9 August at Beirut by Leavitt, who persuaded him to put off his return in view of the delayed but imminent date for action. In these same days, Henderson, officials of the State Department, and officials of the Foreign Office were drafting proposed statements which their governments planned to issue upon the successful conclusion of Ajax.

At Tehran the meetings with the Shah were continuing.

On 2 August Asodollah Rashidian had presented His Majesty with specific details concerning the manner in which the operation would be carried out, and reported that the Shah had agreed to dismiss Mossadeq and to appoint Zahedi as both Prime Minister and Deputy Commander-in-Chief. The Shah also agreed to name General Vosua as Chief of Staff.

On 3 August, Roosevelt had a long and inconclusive session with the Shah. The latter stated that he was not an adventurer and, hence, could not take the chance.

Roosevelt pointed out that there was no other way by which the government could be changed and the test was now between Mossadeq and his force and the Shah and his army, which was still with him, but which would soon slip away.

Roosevelt finally said that he would remain at hand a few days longer in expectation of an affirmative decision and then would leave the country; in the latter case the Shah should realize that failure to act could lead only to a Communist Iran or to a second Korea. He concluded by saying that his government was not prepared to accept these possibilities and that some other plan might be carried through. In a later meeting with the Shah, the latter requested Mr. Roosevelt to solicit from President Eisenhower assurances that it was advisable for the Shah to take the initiative in removing Mossadeq. Mr. Roosevelt stated that he would pass this request on to the President, but he was very confident that the latter would adopt the attitude that the Shah had already had U.S. desires made adequately clear to him. By complete coincidence and good fortune, the President, while addressing the Governors' Convention in Seattle on 4 August, deviated from his script to state by implication that the United States would not sit idly by and see Iran fall behind the Iron Curtain. Mr. Roosevelt used the President's statements to good effect, by telling the Shah that Eisenhower did indeed feel further assurances of U.S. attitude toward Mossadeq were unnecessary but that his reference to Iran in the Governors' Convention speech was made to satisfy the Shah. In the end the Shah said he would again discuss the question with Rashidian.

In the cable describing this meeting, Roosevelt stated his belief that it was hopeless to attempt to proceed without the Shah, and that it must be decided whether to exert ultimate pressure for the next two or three days or to accept a delay of up to ten days in which the Shah might finally be won over. On 7 August Rashidian met again with the Shah who agreed that action should be taken on the night of either the 10th or 11th. On 8 August Roosevelt again saw the Shah and struggled against a mood of stubborn irresolution which broke down to the extent that the Shah agreed to give oral encouragement to selected army officers who would participate in the action. Then, he said, he would go to Ramsar* and let the army act without his official knowledge, adding that if the action was successful he would name Zahedi as Prime Minister. On 9 August Rashidian took over the struggle in his turn and reported that the Shah would leave for Ramsar on the 12th, and that prior to his departure he would see Zahedi and key officers and express orally his choice of Zahedi as the new head of the government.

On 10 August Colonel [Hassan Akhavi] saw the Shah and informed him of the names of the army officers who were ready to take action upon receipt of an order from the Shah. The Shah again asserted that while he approved of the plan for action he would sign no papers. [Akhavi] registered a protest at this decision, and the Shah again sent for Rashidian to discuss this all important point. Rashidian carried a message from Roosevelt to the effect that the latter would leave in complete disgust unless the Shah took action within a few days. At the conclusion of the audience the Shah stated that he would sign the papers, would see Zahedi, and then would leave for Ramsar on the Caspian. The next day he did see Zahedi and did leave for Ramsar, but the papers, contrary to the promise of the Rashidians, were not ready for the

---

* Royal resort on the Caspian Sea, north of Tehran.

signature of the Shah. The Shah thus promised to sign the papers as soon as they were sent to him at Ramsar.

After discussion between Roosevelt and Rashidian, they reverted to a decision closer to the original London draft of Ajax, deciding that there should be two *farmans* royal decrees), one dismissing Mossadeq and one naming Zahedi as Prime Minister. Rashidian and [Behbudi], the Shah's [palace] [head] and an established UK agent, prepared the documents, and on the evening of 12 August [Colonel Nematollah Nasiri], [Commander of the Imperial Guard] took them by plane to Ramsar.

At this time the psychological campaign against Mossadeq was reaching its climax. The controllable press was going all out against Mossadeq, while [REDACTED] under station direction was printing material which the station considered to be helpful. CIA agents gave serious attention to alarming the religious leaders at Tehran by issuing black propaganda in the name of the Tudeh Party, threatening these leaders with savage punishment if they opposed Mossadeq. Threatening phone calls were made to some of them, in the name of the Tudeh, and one of several planned sham bombings of the houses of these leaders was carried out.

The word that the Shah would support direct action in his behalf spread rapidly through the "Colonels' conspiracy" fostered by the station. Zahedi saw station principal agent, Colonel [Aban Farzanegan], and named him as liaison officer with the Americans and as his choice to supervise the staff planning for the action. Then [Farzanegan] took General [Batmangelich] and Colonel [Zand-Karimi] to see Zahedi.

CIA officer Carroll maintained close contact with [Farzanegan] and members of the "Colonels' conspiracy," and on 13 August was present at the final meeting of those individuals to whom would fall the responsibility of carrying out the operational staff plan. However, this meeting was the last one in which the station was represented, and the fact that contact was broken proved to have serious results.

Late on the evening of 13 August, Colonel [Nasiri] returned to Tehran with the *farmans* signed by the Shah and delivered them to

Zahedi; according to his story (which has never been confirmed), it was Queen Soraya [the wife of the Shah] who finally convinced the Shah that he must sign. If this is true, here was an ally from a totally unexpected quarter.

On 14 August the station cabled that upon the conclusion of Ajax the Zahedi government, in view of the empty treasury of the country, would be in urgent need of funds. The sum of $5,000,000 was suggested, and CIA was asked to produce this amount almost within hours after the conclusion of the operation. No more news came in from Tehran on the 14th, and there was nothing that either the station or Headquarters could do except wait for action to begin.

FORMER PRIME MINISTER MOHAMMAD MOSSADEQ'S Minister of Foreign Affairs
Hosseyn Fatemi (standing, dressed in black and with a beard), is shown here in 1954—following the U.S.-backed coup—after he was captured by Savak (the Shah's secret police),
headed at the time by Sardar Moazzam Bakhtiari (seated). Fatemi was an outspoken
Iranian nationalist and supporter of Mossadeq. Fatemi was also an ardent critic of the
Pahlavi monarchy and regularly wrote editorials assailing the royal family. Fatemi was
accused of trying to overthrow the Shah and was sentenced to death. Shortly before he was
executed by firing squad, Fatemi named Mossadeq as the guardian of his only son, Cyrus.

6

THE FIRST TRY

THE PRECISE ORDER OF EVENTS of the night of 15 August 1953 has not yet been established in all details. The early accounts of various participants differed widely enough to make it impossible to follow the slender thread of truth through the dark night. However, the main outline of this first try is clear, as are two basic facts connected with it. These facts are: that the plan was betrayed by the indiscretion of one of the Iranian Army officer participants—primarily because of the protracted delay—and that it still might have succeeded in spite of this advance warning had not most of the participants proved to be inept or lacking in decision at the critical juncture.

Not until the evening of 14 August were Tehran Station personnel informed that action had been postponed from that night until the next one. Station principal agent Colonel [Farzanegan] was no longer in touch with events and the station was unable to guide General [Batmangelich], Zahedi's Chief of Staff designate—if, indeed, it was he who had assumed the main responsibility.

According to a statement by Mossadeq's Chief of Staff, General Tahi Riahi, he was informed of all the details of the "plot" at five in the afternoon of 15 August. But curiously enough—and according to his own account—he did not leave his house in Shimran (the summer resort section north of Tehran) where National Frontists

Zirakzadeh and Haqshenas were staying, until 2000 hours and then drove to staff headquarters in Tehran. Riahi did, however, order the commander of the 1st Armored Brigade to have the brigade ready at 2300 hours. At 2300 hours Riahi sent his deputy, General Kiani, to the Bagh-i-Shah, the army barracks on the western side of Tehran which included the barracks of the Imperial Guard. Kiani was arrested there by Colonel [Nasiri] who had arrived at the Bagh-i-Shah sometime earlier with several officers who supported him. In the meantime a number of truckloads of pro-Shah soldiers were making arrests. About 2330 hours they came to Riahi's house in Shimran and, finding him out, arrested Zirakzadeh and Haqshenas. Also about 2330 hours several officers and a considerable body of soldiers rushed into the home of Hoseyn Fatemi, Mossadeq's Foreign Minister, and took him away before he had a chance to put on his shoes. This meager haul of prisoners was driven to the guard house of the Imperial Palace (Saadabad) at Shimran. Officers who were aware that Riahi had been alerted took no action, but others who were not, carried out their tasks.

Sometime before 2330 hours a limited attack had been made against the telephone system. Wires leading to the house of Fatemi and to the houses of others who were to be arrested were cut; the wires between GHQ (staff headquarters) and the Bagh-i-Shah were cut; and Colonel [REDACTED] with a small armed force, occupied the telephone exchange in the Tehran bazaar.

When Riahi did not hear from General Kiani, who had gone to the Bagh-i-Shah, he (according to his own account) phoned Colonel Momtaz of the 2nd Mountain Brigade and Colonel Shahrokh of the 1st Armored Brigade and told them to take their forces to the Bagh-i-Shah. At or before this time he also alerted other officers, including Colonel Parsa of the 1st Mountain Brigade; Colonel Ashrafi, the Military Governor and Commanding Officer of the 3rd Mountain Brigade; and Colonel Novzari of the 2nd Armored Brigade.

However, according to the accounts of Zahedi men engaged in

their operation, Momtaz and Shahrokh were arrested at the Bagh-i-Shah and held there with Kiani for some time. Government sources differ in their accounts as to what happened when Colonel [Nasiri] tried to deliver to Mossadeq the Shah's *farman* dismissing him. According to General Riahi, Colonel Momtaz was on his way to the Bagh-i-Shah when he ran into Colonel [Nasiri] in the street and thereupon arrested him. According to the official communiqué of the Mossadeq government, [Nasiri] showed up before Mossadeq's house at 0100 hours on 16 August with four trucks full of soldiers, two jeeps, and an armored car. He claimed that he had a letter to deliver to Mossadeq, but was at once arrested by the guards at the house of the Prime Minister. Farzanegan had still another version, claiming that [Nasiri] was arrested at 2350 hours at Mossadeq's house. After his arrest, [Nasiri] is alleged to have said that a delay of two minutes in the arrival at Mossadeq's house of Lt. Colonel [Zand-Karimi] with two truckloads of soldiers caused the plan to fail.

It does seem fairly certain that Riahi had been able before midnight to get detachments of soldiers to the strategic points most likely to be attacked. Just what incident or what reaction on the part of Riahi and others loyal to Mossadeq caused the pro-Zahedi officers to falter in their duties is not clearly known. It is known, however, that Zahedi's Chief of Staff, General [Batmangelich], lost heart and went into hiding. This undoubtedly did much to lower morale at the crucial time, as did the rapidly circulated word of [Nasiri's] arrest. Colonel [Farzanegan] went to the Chief of Staff's office at 0100 hours on the 16th to meet [Batmangelich] and it is known that General [Batmangelich] did approach the GHQ with the intention of taking it over but was frightened off when he saw tanks and troops in readiness. He then rushed to Zahedi and told him to flee, but Zahedi only laughed at him. Even the trucks with the prisoners had come down from Saadabad to the GHQ but, finding it in hostile hands, retreated to Saadabad. Those in charge of the trucks released the prisoners at dawn. Zahedi waited in vain for an escort to come and conduct him to the Officers' Club. By about 0230 hours those Persians who were still willing to carry out the operation were convinced that the cause was lost, as they saw strengthened detachments, more troops moving into the city, and vehicles being stopped for questioning. [Farzanegan] and General [Batmangelich] themselves toured the town about 0230 hours; then presumably separated, since [Batmangelich] was soon picked up, while [Farzanegan] found sanctuary in station hands. At the Embassy the station personnel had spent a nerve-wrecking period of hours. The army radio-equipped jeep called for in the plan failed to arrive at the compound, and there was no way of knowing what was happening in the city.

THE RASHIDIAN BROTHERS

THREE IRANIAN BROTHERS, working closely with British and U.S. intelligence, played pivotal roles in helping to carry out the coup in 1953. Identified throughout the report as "the Rashidians," their names were actually Saifollah, Asadollah and Ghodratollah. The British and the CIA relied heavily on the three because of the contacts they maintained both inside the murky underworld of Iran and among the wealthy elites including the Pahlavi family.

Saifollah, the eldest of the three, was an opium-addicted musician who took great pleasure in philosophy and history. The second brother, Asadollah, was the corpulent and cheery brother who is most often shown in photographs. It was Asadollah who talked the Shah and his sister into participating in the coup. The third brother, Ghodratollah, made his money in investments and kept good connections in the bazaar. This worked out well for the CIA when U.S. agents looked to stir up trouble among the merchants.

In his book on the coup, CIA agent Kermit Roosevelt, the mastermind behind Operation Ajax, named Saifollah and Asadollah as the two Rashidian brothers who were integral to the CIA's plan. Roosevelt trusted Asadollah so much that he had him personally visit the Shah and his sister. The Rashidians also received 10,000 British pounds per month—quite a bit of money at that time—for the purpose of bribing Iranian politicians, religious leaders, street thugs and military officers. As the report later notes, the Rashidians were the ones who orchestrated much of the terrorism and lawlessness on the night the coup was put into place.

THE ABOVE PHOTOGRAPH SHOWING THE SHAH of Iran, Mohammad Reza Pahlavi (right), and General Fazlollah Zahedi (left) was taken in April 1955, a year-and-a-half after the coup. Zahedi was hand-picked by the CIA to take control of the military and the government of Iran following the staged coup because it was believed Zahedi would appear more credible to the Iranian people than had the Shah taken over immediately himself. The CIA believed Zahedi would work with the U.S. and British intelligence and would be willing to turn over power to the Shah after the coup.

7

APPARENT FAILURE

AT 0545 HOURS ON THE MORNING of 16 August 1953, Radio Tehran came on the air with a special government communiqué covering the so-called abortive coup of the night just ending, and by 0600 hours Mossadeq was meeting with his cabinet to receive reports on the situation and to take steps to strengthen the security forces at government buildings and other vital points. Again at 0730 hours the communique was broadcast.

Station personnel had passed an anxious, sleepless night in their office. From the fact that certain actions provided for in the military plan failed to materialize—no jeep with radio arrived at the compound, and the telephone system continued to function—it was obvious that something—or everything—had gone wrong.

At 0500 hours, as soon as the curfew was lifted, Carroll toured the town and reported there was a concentration of tanks and troops around Mossadeq's house, and other security forces on the move. Then Colonel [Farzanegan] called the office to say that things had gone badly, and he, himself, was on the run toward the Embassy in search of refuge. At 0600 hours he appeared, gave a summary of the situation, which was like that of the government communique, and was rushed into hiding. The station was now suddenly faced with the task of rescuing the operation from total failure, and decisions of far-reaching effect were quickly taken. The first need was to establish contact with Ardeshir Zahedi, son of General Zahedi. At 0800 hours he sent word to the station of his whereabouts, and Roosevelt drove up to Shimran to hear that Areshir and his father felt that there was still hope in the situation. It was immediately decided that a strong effort must be made to convince the Iranian public that Zahedi was the legal head of the government and that Mossadeq was the usurper who had staged a coup.

(It should be noted that all action taken from this time on corresponded to the basic estimate of the operational plan that the army would respond to the Shah if they were forced to choose between the ruler and Mossadeq.)

This action was initiated by employing station communications facilities to relay a message to the New York Associated Press (AP) office stating that: "Unofficial reports are current to the effect that leaders of the plot are armed with two decrees of the Shah, one dismissing Mossadeq and the other appointing General Zahedi to replace him." In order to get an authoritative statement that could be distributed for local consumption, the station planned to send General McClure, head of the American Military Mission, to see the Shah and ask him whether the alleged *farman*s were valid. Later in the day it was learned that the Shah had fled.

By 0930 hours the city was calm, with shops opening and people going about their normal business. However, tanks, extra soldiers, and police were stationed at key points, including the royal palaces which were sealed off from outside contact. Rumors began to circulate. The one that gained early attention was to the effect that the alleged coup had been inspired by the government in order to give Mossadeq an excuse to move against the Shah. At about this time Roosevelt sent General McClure to see General Riahi, Chief of Staff, to ask whether the U.S. Military Mission was still accredited to Mossadeq or someone else, as the Embassy had heard that an imperial *farman* had been issued naming Zahedi as Prime Minister. Riahi denied that the *farman* had been "authentically signed" and stated that: "Iran and its people are more important than the Shah or any particular government," and that the army was "of the people and would support the people." It was not until a number of hours later that McClure reported to Roosevelt on this meeting, and from the time of the meeting on, McClure seemed disposed to go along with Riahi in the hope that Riahi himself might eventually try to overthrow Mossadeq.

It was now well into the morning, after the papers had been out for some time. *Shojat*, the substitute for the principal Tudeh paper, *Besuye Ayandeh*, had been predicting a coup since 13 August. It now stated that the plans for the alleged coup had been made after a meeting between the Shah and General Schwarzkopf on 9 August, but that Mossadeq had been tipped off on the 14th.

It should be noted that the Tudeh appeared to be at least as well posted on the coup plans as the government—how is not known. The station principal agent team of [Jalili and Kayvani] working on their own and with singular shrewdness, had put out a special broadsheet which documented the current rumor but twisted it to read that the alleged coup was arranged to force out the Shah. The morning issue of *Mellat-i-Ma* told this same story, while a first mention of the *farman* naming Zahedi was given on an inner page of the large circulation daily *Keyhan*.

At 1000 hours another communiqué added a few details to the earlier one. By this time the Tudeh party members, organized in small groups, were making speeches in many parts of the city, while smaller groups of pro-Mossadeq nationalists were also out in the streets. Then a fresh rumor made the rounds: that a plot had existed but that, when it had failed to materialize, Mossadeq had staged a fake coup.

At 1100 hours two correspondents of the *New York Times* were taken to Shimran, by station arrangement, to see Zahedi. Instead, they saw his son, Ardeshir, who showed them the original of the imperial *farman* naming Zahedi as Prime Minister and gave them photostatic copies.

These photostats had been made by Iranian participants in the plan. Following this meeting the station took charge of the *farman*, had its own photostats made, and kept the original locked up in the station safe until final victory.

At noon Radio Tehran put out a very brief statement signed by Dr. Mohammed Mossadeq (without his title of Prime Minister being used) stating that: "According to the will of the people, expressed by referendum, the 17th Majlis is dissolved. Elections for the 18th session will be held soon." It was this statement, together with the following violently anti-Shah remarks of Fatemi and the undisguised and freely preached republican propaganda of the Tudeh Party, that was instrumental in persuading the general public that Mossadeq was on the verge of eliminating the monarchy.

At 1400 hours Minister of Foreign Affairs Fatemi held a press conference. He stated that for some time past the government had received reports from several sources to the effect that the Imperial Guards were planning a coup and, hence, measures were taken to counteract any such coup. He then went on to review the incidents of the coup, as already stated by government communiques. In reply to a question, he said that Abul Ghassem Amini, Acting Minister of Court, had been arrested since it could not be considered that the court was not a part of the conspiracy. He added that his own views would be found in his editorial in *Bakhtar Emruz*: this editorial, as printed and as read in full, over Radio Tehran at 1730 hours, was a lengthy, malicious attack upon the Shah and upon Reza Shah—a man for whom the general public still feels a large measure of respect and awe. It may be said that this editorial did a great deal to arouse public resentment against the government of Mossadeq.

During the afternoon the station was at work preparing a public statement from General Zahedi which was prepared with the direct advice of Ardeshir Zahedi, the Rashidian brothers, and Colonel [Farzanegan.] When it was ready the agents were unable to find a press in town which was not watched by the government. Therefore, one of the Rashidians did ten copies on a

Persian typewriter. These were rushed to General Zahedi for his signature and then given out to the foreign correspondents, to local pressmen and to two key army officers. By the time they were distributed, it was too late to catch the press for the morning of the 17th. However, station agents, [Jalili and Kayvani] although not in touch with the station, the Rashidians, or [Farzanegan,] went ahead on their own. They composed a fabricated interview with Zahedi and had it printed on the 17th, along with a copy of the *farman*. In this instance, as in a number of others, the high-level agents of the station demonstrated a most satisfying ability to go ahead on their own and do just the right thing.

During the day the station was securing the persons of key individuals and sending them to safety. Some were concealed in the house of a station clerk in the Embassy compound and some in the houses of U.S. personnel of the station outside the compound. Thus, Ardeshir Zahedi was in station hands from the morning of the 16th on, General Zahedi from the morning of the 17th on, the Rashidian brothers from the 16th on with the exception of a venture out on the 18th, Colonel [Farzanegan] from the morning of the 16th on, and General [Guilanshah] from the morning of the 16th. These people had to be concealed by the station, both in order to secure them from arrest and also to have them in places to which Americans could logically and easily go.

That evening, about 1930 hours, crowds massed in the Majlis Square to hear speeches, and the proceedings were rebroadcast over Radio Tehran. The speakers included pro-Mossadeq ex-Majlis deputies Mosavi, Dr. Szyyid Ali Shayegan, Engineer Zirakzadeh, Engineer Razavi, and Foreign Minister Fatemi. All the speakers attacked the Shah and demanded that he abdicate. During the course of these speeches, the public was informed for the first time that the Shah had fled to Baghdad. The station had learned several hours earlier that the Shah had left. By 1600 hours the two principal U.S. Embassy political officers had given up hope, while Roosevelt was insisting there was still a "slight remaining chance of success" if the Shah would use the Baghdad radio and if Zahedi took an aggressive stand.

Additional station messages to Headquarters contained the texts of the type of statements the Shah could make over Baghdad radio.

Allowing for the seven hour difference in time, Headquarters received the first message from the station on the non-success of the coup at 0130 hours on the 16th, and a few hours thereafter was working on the station's request to get the Shah to broadcast from Baghdad. As the working day ended, they had to report to the station that the State Department was firmly opposed to any American effort to contact the Shah and suggested the British do it. At Nicosia they responded enthusiastically to the station's suggestion, and the SIS attempted to get permission from London to have Leavitt and Darbyshire flown to Baghdad by RAF jet fighter early in the morning of the 17th, for the purpose of exerting pressure on the Shah. London refused permission.

As the station personnel entered on another day after a second sleepless night, some real encouragement came from word that, in breaking up Tudeh groups late the night before, the soldiers had beaten them with rifle butts and made them shout, "Long live the Shah." The station continued to feel that the "project was not quite dead" since General Zahedi, General [Guilanshah], the Rashidian brothers, and Colonel [Farzanegan] were still determined to press action.

Now, on the morning of 17 August, the press was again on the streets. *Niruye Sevum* stated that Schwarzkopf engineered the plot with the Shah and that "simple-minded Americans thought the Shah was a trump card." *Dad* and *Shahed* both blamed the so-called coup on the government, and *Keyhan* carried the text of an alleged Radio London statement quoting Zahedi to the effect that he had a *farman* from the Shah and that the Shah had left because his life was threatened.

Throughout the morning Iranians with good radios were able to get word from foreign stations of statements that the Shah had made in Baghdad. He said: "What has taken place in Iran cannot be considered a coup d'etat in the real sense."

The Shad said he had issued his orders for the dismissal of Dr. Mossadeq under the prerogatives given to him by the constitution, and had appointed General Zahedi in his place. He went on to say that he had not abdicated and that he was confident of the loyalty of the Iranian people to him. This line was what the station had in mind, if less strong than desired; and the Baghdad papers hinted that painful, bloody events were still to come in Iran.

The station suggested that Imam Khalasi, religious divine at Baghdad, and the Agha Khan be enlisted to give the Shah moral backing, while Headquarters, on State Department instructions, continued to refuse permission for direct U.S. contact with the Shah. In the meantime the U.S. Ambassador to Iraq, Burton Berry, reported on his conversation with the Shah on the evening of the 16th. His statements, made on his own initiative, were quite in line with suggestions reaching him after the event.

About 1000 hours a considerable body of the troops that had been dispersed throughout the city were called back to their barracks, as the government was certain the situation was well in hand. At 1030 hours Radio Tehran called up General Zahedi to surrender to the authorities, and then began broadcasting lists of those arrested as having taken part in the abortive coup or having had some connection with those events. The separate lists, including those of the next day, contained the following names (those underlined indicate the individuals who were known to the station to be engaged in the coup attempt):

[Acting Minister of Court Abul Ghassem Amini Colonel Novzari,]

[Commander of 2nd Armored Brigade Colonel Zand-Karimi,]

[Chief of Staff of 2nd Mountain Brigade Commander Poulad Daj of the Police Colonel Nematollah Nasiri,]

[Commander of Imperial Guards Lt. Colonel Azamudeh,]

[Reg. CO 1st Mountain Brigade Colonel Parvaresh,]
[Head of the Officers' Club 1st Lieutenant Niahi Mr. Perron,]
[Swiss subject <u>General Nadr Batmangelich</u>,]
[Retired Colonel Hadi Karayi,]
[Commander of Imperial Guards at Namsar General Shaybani,]
[Retired Rahim Hirad,]
[Chief of Shah's private secretariat <u>Soleiman Behbudi</u>,]
[Chief of Shah's household <u>Lt. Colonel Hamidi</u>,]
[Asst. Director of Police visa section Colonel Mansurpur,]
[Squadron Leader (cavalry) Colonel Rowhani,]
[Chief of Staff of 3rd Mountain Brigade Captain Baladi 1st Lieutenant Naraghi Captain Shaghaghi Captain Salimi]
[1st Lieutenant Eskandari]
[1st Lieutenant Jafarbey]
[Mr. Ashtari]
[Mr. Mohammed Jehandari]
[1st Lieutenant Rauhani]
[Dr. Mozaffar Baqai]

Rumors circulated to the effect that the arrested officers were to be hanged on 20 August, and throughout the unit commands of the Tehran garrison, the police, and the gendarmerie, officers met to discuss the situation. Several of them resolved to risk all to attempt to rescue their friends.

The station devoted a great deal of effort during the day to circulating photostatic copies of the *farman*—particularly among the army—and in trying to arrange for more and more press coverage. It was now obvious that public knowledge of the existence of the *farman*s was having an effect. Everyone was asking questions:

"Was it true that the Shah had issued the *farman*s? If so, why was Mossadeq lying about it? Wasn't that a most reprehensible thing to do?"

At 1325 hours Fatemi held a press conference at which he dealt with the flight of the Shah to Iraq, read the abjectly pleading letter from arrested Acting Minister of Court Armini, and stated that 14 officers had been arrested.

His more detailed views on the current situation were expressed in an editorial in *Bakhtar Emruz* and were in the main a repetition of his previous scurrilous attacks against the Shah. He wrote such words as, "O traitor Shah, you shameless person, you have completed the criminal history of the Pahlavi reign. The people . . . want to drag you from behind your desk to the gallows."

Early in the afternoon, Ambassador Henderson arrived in Tehran from Beirut. On the way out to the airport to meet him, members of the Embassy passed the site of the bronze statue of Reza Shah at the end of the avenue of that name. Only the boots of the figure remained on the pedestal. A passing truck was dragging behind it the horse from the equestrian statue of the same ruler that had stood in Sepah Square. In the crowds engaged in this activity, the Tudeh were obviously in the majority.

On behalf of the government, Henderson was welcomed by Dr. Gholam Hosein Mossadeq, son of the Prime Minister, and by Dr. Alemi, Minister of Labor. At 1630 hours the station sent off a cable giving a general survey of the local situation which, although it foresaw Mossadeq's position strengthened for the next few weeks, did insist that a policy of opposition to him be continued. Near the end of the afternoon, the government used the voice of a religious leader, Sadr Balaghi, to attack the Shah over Radio Tehran.

The evening was a most active and trying time for the station. Principal agents [Kayvani and Jalili] were reached and given instructions. Within the Embassy compound, Roosevelt and Carroll held a prolonged council of war with the heads of their team: General Zahedi and Ardeshir Zahedi, General [Guilanshah,] the Rashidian brothers, and Colonel [Farzanegan]. These teammates were, when required, smuggled in and out of the compound in the bottom of cars and in closed jeeps. A few hundred yards away Ambassador Henderson and General McClure were out in the garden in front of the residency, and Roosevelt wore a path back and forth to reassure them that no Persians were hidden out in the compound, so that they could in all honesty so inform Mossadeq if the question were asked. The council of war went on for about four hours, and in the end it was decided that some action would be taken on Wednesday the 19th.

As preparation for this effort, several specific activities were to be undertaken. In the field of political action, it was planned to send the Tehran cleric [Ayatollah Behbehani] to Qum to try to persuade the supreme cleric, Ayatollah Borujerdi, to issue a *fatwa* (religious decree) calling for a holy war against Communism, and also to build up a great demonstration on Wednesday on the theme that it was time for loyal army officers and soldiers and the people to rally to the support of religion and the throne. In the field of military action, support from outside of Tehran seemed essential. Colonel [Farzanegan] was sent off in a car driven by a station agent (U.S. national Gerald Towne) to [Kermanshah, a distance of 400 miles,] to persuade Colonel [Timur Bakhtiar,] commanding officer of the [Kermanshah] garrison, to declare for the Shah. Zahedi, with Carroll, was sent to Brigadier General [Zargham] at [Isfahan] with a similar request. Through station facilities these messengers were provided with identification papers and travel papers which stood up under inspection. All those leaving the compound were also given station-prepared curfew passes.

Throughout the long hours of 17 August, there seemed little that Headquarters could do to ease the pangs of despair. A wire sent to the station in the afternoon expressed the strong feeling that Roosevelt, in the interest of safety, should leave at the earliest moment, and it went on to express distress over the bad luck. At about the same time, an operational immediate cable went out to Ambassador Berry in Baghdad with guidance concerning his future meetings with the Shah.

Propaganda guidance was sent to the stations in Karachi, New Delhi, Cairo, Damascus, Istanbul, and Beirut to the effect that the Zahedi government was the only legal one. Just after midnight Headquarters urged a Paris Station officer in southern France to get in touch with the Agha Khan [the billionaire spiritual leader of Shia Muslims and a direct descendent of Mohammad through the prophet's daughter, Fatima] at once, in order to urge the latter to send a wire to the Shah expressing his strongest moral support. Much later, Headquarters learned that contact had been established, but there was not the hoped-for outcome.

The Agha Khan had at once stated that a ruler who left his throne and country would never return, and after his statement no effort was made to sell him on the idea of backing the Shah. Of course, he was later delighted to hear that the Shah did get his throne back after all.

At Nicosia the SIS refused to give up hope, and bucked against their own office in London and against the Foreign Office. Darbyshire continued to try to get permission to go to Baghdad. While the persistence and apparent faith shown by the SIS station at Nicosia was altogether admirable, it should be remembered that they had nothing to lose if the cause had been pressed to ultimate failure and disclosure.

The 18th was to be the most trying day for every person in every country who was aware of the project. At 0730 hours that morning the Shah left Baghdad for Rome on a regular BOAC [British Overseas Airways Corporation] commercial flight. It would be some hours before this news reached Tehran. In Tehran the day opened with small bands roaming the streets. The Tudeh managed to ransack the Pan-Iranist Party headquarters ([Kayvani/Jalili] claim credit for this incident) located near the Majlis Square, and then there were minor clashes between gangs of the Tudeh and the Third Force (a Marxist, non-Tudeh opposition group).

Morning papers appeared about as usual, although very few

opposition sheets were available since secret police were posted in all printing shops. Those papers supporting Mossadeq announced that the the Pahlavi dynasty had come to an end, while [*Ettelaat* (despite assurances from its publisher to support the station's line)] wrote that the nation expressed its violent disapproval of the coup which was in foreign interests. [*Dad* continued its really remarkable efforts by reprinting the *farman* and an interview with Zahedi.] *Shahed* ran a copy of the *farman*, and *Keyhan* ran two brief notes on Zahedi's claims. *Shojat*, replacement for *Besuye Ayandeh* and, hence, the leading organ of the Tudeh Party, printed a statement by the Central Committee of the Tudeh Party—the first such statement to appear for some weeks. In this statement the party blamed the recent events on Anglo-American intrigue, and added that the watchword for the day must be: ". . . Down with the monarchy! Long live the democratic republic!" During the morning the AP correspondent wired out a story, destined to get considerable play abroad, which included Zahedi's statement to the officers of the Iranian Army: "Be ready for sacrifice and loss of your lives for the maintenance of independence and of the monarchy of Iran and of the holy religion of Islam which is now being threatened by infidel Communists."

Military communiques read over Radio Tehran indicated that continuing efforts were being made by the government to firm up its control. One announcement offered a reward of 100,000 rials for information as to the whereabouts of General Zahedi, [a second demanded that retired officer Colonel Abat Farzanegan appear before the military government] and a third was a reminder that all demonstrations were forbidden by the government.

At 1030 hours General Riahi, Chief of Staff, met with the high-ranking officers of the army in the lecture hall of the Military School and read them the riot act, stressing that they must be faithful to the government.

Personnel at the Tehran Station, while continuing to make every effort to carry out its decision of the 16th, were also planning for eventualities. One message to Headquarters asked that the means for a clandestine evacuation of up to 15 people from Iran be prepared. Another cited local military opinion that officers would carry out instructions broadcast by the Shah, and then went on to put it up to Headquarters as to whether the station should continue with Ajax or withdraw. Nicosia commiserated over the initial failure and stated that they, personally, were continuing to do all they could to induce London to continue to support station efforts.

This message was followed by a report on the Shah's statements at Baghdad, and by still another to the effect that SIS Nicosia was asking London's assent to urge the Shah's return on pilgrimage to the holy shrines in Iraq where he would be in direct contact with Iranian residents there.

During the afternoon most of the news was not of action but of statements from various sources. At his press conference Minister of Foreign Affairs Fatemi asserted that there had been serious anti-Shah riots in Baghdad—a complete lie.

At 1500 hours the Shah arrived in Rome, where he was to make statements to the press which followed a middle ground. These statements did not dash the hopes of his supporters, but neither were they a call to action.

Also, in the afternoon, Radio Moscow carried the text of the appeal of the Central Committee of the Tudeh Party as it had been printed that morning in *Shojat*.

In the evening, violence flared in the streets of Tehran. Just what was the major motivating force is impossible to say, but it is possible to isolate the factors behind the disturbances.

First, the flight of the Shah brought home to the populace in a dramatic way how far Mossadeq had gone, and galvanized the people into an irate pro-Shah force.

Second, it seems clear that the Tudeh Party overestimated its strength in the situation. This fault may have been that of the Soviet liaison people, or of the leaders of the Tudeh Party, or of the rank and file. During the day the party not only had defiled statues of the monarchy, but also had erected their own flags at certain points. Party members had also torn down street signs in which the Pahlavi dynasty was mentioned or which commemorated events in the reign of Reza Shah, and had replaced them with "popular" names. The party seemed ready for an all-out effort to bring in a peoples' democracy, believing either that Mossadeq would not challenge them or that they could outfight him in the streets.

Third, the Mossadeq government was at last beginning to feel very uneasy about its alliance with the Tudeh Party. The Pan-Iranists were infuriated and the Third Force was most unhappy about the situation.

Fourth, the climax was now approaching of the [Kayvani/Jalili] campaign of alleged Tudeh terrorism. (Details of this campaign have been given on earlier pages.) On this evening [Kayvani/Jalili] had gangs of alleged Tudehites on the streets with orders to loot and smash shops on Lalezar and Amirieh streets whenever possible, and to make it clear that this was the Tudeh in action.

During the evening all these factors came together. Security forces were given orders to clear the streets and serious fighting resulted. Friends of Colonel [Hamidi] in the Police Department exceeded instructions in preventing Tudeh vandalism by beating up Tudehites and shouting for the Shah.

The Tudeh did seem to take rapid cognizance of the facts that a covert action was being staged, and that their members were not strong enough to fight the police. They brought people out who tried to argue demonstrators into going home.

Headquarters spent a day featured by depression and despair. The immediate direction of the project moved from the Branch and Division to the highest level. At the end of the morning a handful of people worked on the draft of a message which was to call off the operation.

As the message was finally sent, in the evening, it was based on the Department of State's tentative stand: "that the operation has been tried and failed," the position of the United Kingdom that: "we must regret that we cannot consider going on fighting"

and Headquarters' position that, in the absence of strong recommendations to the contrary from Roosevelt and Henderson,
operations against Mossadeq should be discontinued.

ON AUG. 19, 1953, SOLDIERS SURROUNDED THE PARLIAMENT, or Majlis, building in Tehran, believing that they were acting for the good of Iran under orders from the Shah. In fact, the CIA had manipulated the entire situation. The night before the actual coup took place, CIA and British agents had been staging violent attacks with street gangs posing as Mossadeq supporters in order to set up groups such as the Tudeh Party and to implicate Mossadeq in the destruction and looting.

8

THE SHAH IS VICTORIOUS

WHILE ON THE 18TH ONLY [Dr. Baghai's paper *Shahed*] had published the imperial *farman* naming Zahedi as Prime Minister, on 19 August, as soon as the city was awake, early risers could see photostats or type-set copies of the *farman* in the papers *Setareh Islam, Asia Javanan, Aram, Mard-i-Asia, Mellat-i-Ma*, and the *Journal de Tehran*. The first four of these papers, and *Shahed* and *Dad* in addition, ran an alleged interview with Zahedi which stressed that his government was the only legal one in existence—an interview that had been fabricated by [Jalili]. Somewhat later in the morning the first of many thousand of broadsheets which carried a photo-static copy of the *farman* and the text of the Zahedi statement appeared in the streets. Although each of these newspapers had a normal circulation of restricted size, the news they carried was undoubtedly flashed through the city by word of mouth, for before 0900 hours pro-Shah groups were assembling in the bazaar area. Members of these groups had not only made their personal choice between Mossadeq and the Shah, but they were stirred up by the Tudeh activity of the preceding day and were ready to move. They needed only leadership.

Even before the day had dawned [Kayvani and Jalili] having been informed that a pro-Shah statement by the ranking religious leader, Ayatollah Borujerdi, might be forthcoming during the day, had made definite preparations to utilize any such statement. [Jalili] and two of their most energetic sub-agents, [Mansur Afshar and Majidi] were down at the bazaar section with a jeep and trucks ready to set out for Qazvin. Their plan was to print broadsheets at this town some 85 miles west of Tehran should it appear that the Mossadeq government had increased its attempted stranglehold on the urban press. As soon as they noticed that the pro-Shah groups were gathering, [Jalili, Majidi,] [and Rezali, another sub-agent] rushed to supply the needed leadership. [Jalili] accompanied one group in its progress toward the Majlis, and on the way incited them to set fire to the offices of *Bakhtar-i-Emruz*, the semi-official paper owned by Minister of Foreign Affairs Fatemi, which on the 17th and 18th had printed bitter and scurrilous attacks on the person of the Shah. About the same time [Afshar] led other elements toward the offices of the Tudeh papers *Shahbaz*, *Besuye Ayandeh*, and *Javanan-i-Democrat*, all of which were thoroughly sacked.

The news that something quite startling was happening spread at great speed throughout the city. Just when it reached Mossadeq, who was meeting with members of his cabinet, is not known. By 0900 hours the station did have this news, and by 1000 hours word had come in that both the *Bakhtar-i-Emruz* office and the headquarters of the Iran Party had been ransacked. Also, about 1000 hours, contact was established with the Rashidian brothers who seemed full of glee. Their instructions, as well as orders directed to [Kayvani and Jalili], were now to attempt to swing security forces to the side of the demonstrators and to encourage action for the capture of Radio Tehran. To what extent the resulting activity stemmed from specific efforts of all our agents will never be known, although many more details of the excitement of the day may slowly come to light.

Fairly early in the morning Colonel [Demavand] one of those involved in the staff planning, appeared in the square before the Majlis with a tank which he had secured from the Second Battalion of the Second Armored Brigade, [a battalion] [originally committed to the operation] Lt. Col. [Khosro Panah] and Captain [Ali Zand] were on hand and were joined by two trucks from the same battalion, while members of the disbanded Imperial Guard seized trucks and drove through the streets. By 1015 hours there were pro-Shah truckloads of military personnel at all the main squares.

While small groups had penetrated to the north of the city by 0930 hours, the really large groups, armed with sticks and stones, came from south Tehran and merged as they reached Sepah Square in their progress north toward the center of the city. There the troops, held in readiness, fired hundreds of shots over the heads of the crowd, but apparently were not willing to fire at these partisans of the Shah. As a result the crowds were able to fan out toward key points. Just up Lalezar, a main shopping street, the Saadi theater, long sponsored by the Tudeh Party, was burned. The surging crowds of men, women, and children were shouting, "*Shah piruz ast,*" (The Shah is victorious).

Determined as they seemed, a gay holiday atmosphere prevailed, and it was if exterior pressures had been released so that the true sentiments of the people showed through. The crowds were not, as in earlier weeks, made up of hoodlums, but included people of all classes—many well dressed—led or encouraged by other civilians. Trucks and busloads of cheering civilians streamed by and when, about noon, five tanks and 20 truckloads of soldiers joined it, the movement took on a somewhat different aspect. As usual, word spread like lightning and in other parts of the city pictures of the Shah were eagerly display. Cars went by with headlights burning as a tangible indication of loyalty to the ruler.

At about 1030 hours, General Riahi informed Mossadeq that he no longer controlled the army and asked for relief, but Mossadeq visited his office and told him to hold firm. Colonel Momtaz was able to assemble only one battalion and disposed that force around Mossadeq's house. About noon separate elements composing the crowds began to receive direct leadership from the military and police. Those army officers previously alerted to take part in the military operations provided by Ajax were now taking separate but proper individual action. By 1300 hours the central headquarters of the telegraph office on Sepah Square had fallen into royalist hands. The AP man filed a cable there shortly after 1300 hours giving a brief report on the fighting. Then fighting moved a few hundred yards away to the police headquarters and to the Ministry of Foreign Affairs building just across the wide avenue from it. Defenders of the police station held out until nearly 1600 hours.

Also about noon, Roosevelt went to the houses where Generals Zahedi and [Guilanshah] were in hiding. They were both fully informed of the events of the morning and told to wait for instructions. An hour later Carroll and Persian-speaking Major William R. Keyser (Assistant U.S. Military Attache) reported on the military situation. By early afternoon more of the important objectives in the center of the city, such as the press and propaganda offices, had been taken over by the royalists. With important facilities under control, it was possible to begin dispatch of streams of telegrams to the provinces urging them to rise in support of the Shah. Even during the greatest heat of the day there was no slackening of activity. Station agent [Jalili] was still on the streets and, finding a crowd on Firdausi Avenue, urge them to go to military police headquarters and demand the release of Colonel [Nasiri] and General [Batmanlegich]. This they did. The soldiers on guard put up no resistance. Meanwhile agent General [Nakhi Qods Nakhai] was touring the city in his car attempting to round up members of the Imperial Guard, soldiers who later took part in the attack on Mossadeq's house. Early in the afternoon the crowds did collect around approaches to Mossadeq's residence. By this time he had probably already left.

Radio Tehran was a most important target, for its capture not only sealed the success at the capital, but was effective in bringing the provincial cities quickly into line with the new government. During the heat of activity, it broadcast dull discussions of cotton prices, and finally music only. Already at 1030 hours there had been an interruption of its schedule, but it was not until early afternoon that people began streaming up the broad avenue toward their goal, some three miles to the north. Buses and trucks bore full loads of civilians, army officers and policemen. Sheer weight of numbers seemed to have overwhelmed the defenders of the radio station, and after a brief struggle in which three deaths were reported, at 1412 hours the station was in royalist hands. At 1420 hours it broadcast the first word of the success of the royalist effort, including a reading of the *farman*. A stream of eager speakers came to the microphone. Some represented elements upon whom reliance had been placed in Ajax planning, while others were quite unknown to the station. Among the former elements were opposition papers [*Bakhtiar* and *Zelzeleh*,] one of [Ayatollah Kashani's sons,] and [Likeh Etozadi]. Among spontaneous supporters of the Shah to come to the microphone were Colonel Ali Pahlevan and Major Huband Mirzadian; their presence was the proof—no longer required—of the truth of the Ajax assumption that the army would rally to the Shah under just such circumstances. For some period of time, Radio Tehran was alternately on and off the air. It may have been finally put into good operating condition by those engineers who, as one speaker said, had come along for just such a purpose.

Here, as in so many other phases, chance served the cause very well, for, had the original defenders of the radio station managed to damage its facilities, the firm control of the capital might have been delayed.

At the Embassy, station personnel were following the broadcasts of Radio Tehran, and were elated when it suddenly fell into royalist hands. Once again Roosevelt set off toward the hiding place of his valuable charges, meeting them a little before 1600 hours. Told it was time for them to play an active role, both promptly dressed for the occasion. It was agreed that General Zahedi should meet General [Guilanshah] at 1630 hours on a certain street corner with a tank, and should proceed with this vehicle to Radio Tehran where Zahedi would speak to the nation. General [Guilanshah] was taken from the house by Major [Keyser] in a jeep; and then along the way, he spied two Air Force officers, he asked to be let out, saying he would take care of everything. Right on the street these officers greeted him warmly and when he said he would like a tank, they soon rounded one up. Asked if he knew where Zahedi was, he said he did and that he had an appointment to meet him at 1630 hours. His comrades pressured him to make an immediate rendezvous with Zahedi, so he directed the tank toward the compound in which the house sheltering Zahedi was situated. Zahedi emerged and the tank set off again. At 1725 hours Zahedi spoke over Radio Tehran, and this speech was repeated a little after 2100 hours that evening.

However, Zahedi had been preceded on the air by [station agent Farzanegan]. In the dash back from [Karmenshah] [Farzanegan's] car had broken down completely at about the halfway mark, but he was able to get an uncomfortable ride the rest of the way in an oil tank truck. He arrived in Tehran by morning and contacted the station. At the latter's urgent instructions, [Farzanegan] sent a telegram to Colonel [Bakhtiar] which message contained a code phrase* signaling [Bakhtiar] to lead his division on forced march to Tehran.

An interesting sidelight concerning [Bakhtiar's] march to Tehran** occurred en route to Hamadan. The division entered Hamadan just as the local Tudeh Party was holding a large pro-Mossadeq demonstration. [Bakhtiar] quelled the demonstration in short order. The astonishment of the Tudeh on seeing the [Kermanshah] division enter Hamadan was exceeded only by that of the town mayor.

Within Tehran proper the last nests of resistance were being subdued. The Chief of Staff headquarters gave in at the end of the afternoon, and before 1900 hours Mossadeq's house was taken and soon turned into a shambles. Its belongings were dragged out into the street and sold to passersby. Reactions were also being reported from the provinces. At 1450 hours the regional station at Sanandaj in Kurdestan suddenly went off the air. At 1555 hours Radio Tabriz reported the capture of the station itself by forces

---

* "Am coming today to see my sick sister."

** The division actually arrived after Tehran was already in royalist hands.

THE SHAH IS VICTORIOUS 73

loyal to the Shah, and stated that all of Azerbaijan was in the hands of the army. As it continued broadcasting, it became apparent that one of the speakers, [Mohammad Deyhim, head of the Fedakaran-i-Azerbaijan] and an effective sub-agent of station assets had played an important role in events at Tabriz. By 1800 hours the station at Isfahan was on the air with strong statements in favor of the Shah and Zahedi by such elements as local editors, a member of Baghai's Toiler's Party, religious leaders, and staff officers—all groups which we had hoped would react in this fashion. Not until 2000 hours did the radio station at Kerman proclaim loyalty to the new government. Meshed Radio was not heard from at all, but the religious-minded town turned loyalist almost immediately after the news of the change had been sent out over Radio Tehran. Known Tudehites were pursued and shops of Tudeh sympathizers looted.

Colonel [Farzanegan] following Zahedi's instruction, and Carroll now closed up the operation. While [Batmangelich] had [been named chief of staff, Farzanegan]—at that office—kept in touch by phone and placed known supporters of Ajax in command of all units of the Tehran garrison, seized key military targets, and executed the arrest lists. As the afternoon drew to its close, Radio Tehran seemed to get down to a less haphazard schedule. From 1800 hours on, it made short announcements of government appointees. At 1845 hours the Associated Press representative and *The New York Times* man made fairly brief statements on the events of the day, intended for their home offices. Brief government communiques dealt with curfew hours, contained warnings against demonstrations, etc. A general news summary at 2100 hours was followed by a statement from Zahedi, installed in the office of the Chief of Police, and before 2200 hours the station had signed off for the night. The hectic day was over and curfew now in effect. Lives had been lost, but not nearly as many as stated in the white heat of the actual events. The security forces were firmly in control and well prepared to destroy any counter-effort.

How had other interested parties weathered the exciting day? One such must have felt real anguish. This was the USSR and its people in Iran. Radio Moscow lagged far behind the rest of the world and did not put out a summary of the day's events at Tehran until 2300 hours GMT. Its Persian program that reached Iran early in the afternoon was built around the text of the earlier *Pravda* article entitled "The Failure of the American Adventure in Iran," and this program was repeated early in the evening. The same *Pravda* article was broadcast throughout the late afternoon and early evening from Moscow in English, Arabic, Bulgarian, Polish, Czech and Slovak, German, Dutch, Italian, Portuguese, and Turkish, although by that time nearly every one of its listeners must have known that this material was no longer applicable.

The other parties to the original plan felt elated, and possibly self-satisfied. While the reactions of the Shah at Rome are rather beyond the scope of this account, one or two of his remarks are worth citing as they bear upon some of the original assumptions of the Ajax plan.

He said, "It was my people who have shown me that they were faithful to the monarchy and that two and a half years of false propaganda were not enough," and again, "My country didn't want the Communists and therefore have been faithful to me."

At Nicosia the earliest FBI intercepts had not been translated and distributed until nearly mid-afternoon local time. As word passed from Leavitt to Darbyshire, the latter became so excited that he drove his friend right to his office outside of the town, something he and his associates had always avoided doing in earlier weeks.

Headquarters had its first word of what the day was to bring just before 0900 hours when someone burst in from the hall pouring out what at first seemed to be a bad joke—in view of the depression that still hung on from the day before—the news that Mossadeq was on the way out.

Throughout the morning, the afternoon, and until late that night people hurried down the corridors with fresh slips of ticker tape.

During the entire day only two Ajax cables were received from the station. However, it was a day that should never have ended for it carried with it such a sense of excitement, of satisfaction, and of jubilation that it is doubtful whether any other can come up to it. Our trump card had prevailed and the Shah was victorious.

THE ABOVE PHOTOGRAPH SHOWS A YOUNG Mohammad Reza Pahlavi saluting Winston Churchill on the occasion of Churchill's 69th birthday at the close of the Tripartite Conference of Tehran in November 1943. Churchill, acting on behalf of the Anglo-Iranian Oil Company, wanted Mossadeq and the "National Frontists" out of Iran's government, following Mossadeq's call to nationalize Iran's oil.

9

REPORT TO LONDON

ROOSEVELT ARRIVED IN LONDON the afternoon of 25 August. He had been smuggled out of Tehran in Naval Attache Eric Pollard's plane and picked up by a Military Air Transport Service (MATS) plane (the pilot and crew of which were not aware of his identity) at Bahrain. In London Roosevelt was met by Firth and taken to see Maj. General J. Alexander Sinclair and others in SIS that evening. From the very beginning it was made plain to him that SIS was grateful not only because of the success of the operation per se, but because of the effect its success had already had and would continue to have upon SIS's reputation and relations with its superiors. In turn he expressed gratitude for the fine support the station had received and recognition of the fact that such weaknesses as had existed in the support given us were attributable to the paucity of reporting from Tehran, which had resulted in a justifiable lack of hope both in London and Washington. Roosevelt went to some pains to explain the reason for the lack of reporting. He pointed out that if they had simply reported what they were doing, London and Washington would have thought they were crazy and told them to stop immediately; if they had reported the reasons why they felt justified in taking such action they would have had no time to take action; accordingly, they followed the third course which was to act, and report practically nothing. This decision was initially made on the assumption that they had very little more to lose by following up the last hopes, and everything to win. As the hours passed, evidence that the action had great hopes of success increased rapidly, but they still had no time or energy to prepare and present the evidence. Sinclair and members of his staff said that they fully understood the situation and were glad that Roosevelt had taken what was in their opinion the best and most constructive decision. We all recognized, however, that if the outcome had been different, a substantially different attitude toward that action might have been found in many quarters. Sinclair commented that it was recognition of the probability that such grave decisions would have to be taken speedily and could only be taken in the field that had led him to request the appointment of a combined theater commander. He also requested that in Roosevelt's briefing of senior members of the British Foreign Office he should emphasize this aspect of the story. The following days Roosevelt did so, and, without exception, from Churchill through Lord Salisbury all down the line, the decision taken in Tehran was enthusiastically endorsed. (Sir Winston made reference to Lord Nelson's blind eye.)

On 26 August Roosevelt was shepherded through a round of appointments at the Foreign Offices by the Foreign Office representative attached to SIS. He first saw Sir (Reginald) James Bowker (Byroade's British opposite number—responsible for NEA) and two members of his staff, and gave them an account of developments and the psychological climate in Iran, without giving much in the way of operational detail. He got the impression that SIS was glad to take advantage of any opportunity of selling themselves to this level of the Foreign Office. It appeared that their relationship, at least in this area, were neither close nor cordial at this level. Later in the morning he spent an hour alone with the Acting Foreign Secretary, Lord Salisbury. As requested by Sinclair, Roosevelt gave Lord Salisbury the full treatment, and he appeared to be absolutely fascinated. His attitude seemed to be very much more flexible and progressive that that of Bowker. He seemed genuinely anxious to help the new Iranian Government and very con-

scious of the problems which the relations with the United
Kingdom presented to that government. He recognized the importance of immediate short-term economic aid which would produce
quick and obvious results, but remarked that perhaps long-range
aid could be worked out with an "oil settlement in mind."
Roosevelt reported fully to Salisbury, as he had to Bowker, on the
assurances which he had given on behalf of Her Majesty's
Government (HMG) to the Shah and Zahedi. Salisbury assured
him, as did everyone else, that those statements were justified and
properly presented, that the British fully appreciated the necessity of reaching agreement on an oil settlement with the Iran
Government as rapidly as possible, and that they were fully prepared to do so.

At 1400 hours Roosevelt was received by the Prime Minister
who was in bed at 10 Downing Street. This was a most touching
occasion. The Prime Minister seemed to be in bad shape physi-
cally. He had great difficulty in hearing; occasional difficulty in
articulating; and apparent difficulty seeing to his left. In spite of
this he could not have been more kind personally nor more enthu-
siastic about the operation.

He was good enough to express envy of Roosevelt's role and a
wish that he had been "some years" younger and might have
served under his command. He repeated the statement that he had
already made to Sinclair, that if the success of this operation could
be maintained it would be the finest operation since the end of the
war. He emphasized his strong feeling that everything possible to
help the new government should be done. Economic aid to Iran
should not wait either for the restoration of diplomatic relations
with the British or for an oil settlement.

He went so far as to proclaim that if it were necessary he, himself, would provide economic aid to Iran before the restoration of
diplomatic relations, although he did not explain how this might
be accomplished. He commented that the Anglo-Iranian Oil
Company (AIOC) had really "fouled things up" in the past few
years and that he was determined that they should not be allowed
to foul things up any further. Our operation had given us a won-

derful and unexpected opportunity which might change the whole picture in the Middle East. In closing he asked Roosevelt to tell the President that he was feeling much better and could "hang on as long as may be necessary." He also asked that Roosevelt write to him after his meeting with the President, and that he keep in touch with him in the future.

The Prime Minister made several references which indicated that he regarded SIS as his service, and that it was very close to his heart. Perhaps due to his physical condition at the time, however, he appeared a bit hazy as to its jurisdiction and the distinction between MI-5 and MI-6.

He was definitely hazy on Sinclair and upon the American setup. The initials CIA meant nothing to him, but he had a vague idea that Roosevelt must be connected in some way with his old friend Bedell Smith.

At the outset Sinclair had said that he thought it might make a better impression if neither he nor any member of his service were present during Roosevelt's reports to other members of HMG, and although he knew that Roosevelt was to see the Prime Minister and the Acting Foreign Secretary, he suggested only one exception to this procedure. He asked if Roosevelt would have any objection to his sitting in on the discussions with Sir William Strang, the Permanent Under Secretary for Foreign Affairs. He explained that Strang was the source of his political guidance and such authorizations as were required from the Foreign Office, and said that he was anxious to see the impact of certain portions of this briefing upon Strang.

In the course of the conversations it became apparent that the portion of particular interest to Sinclair was the reason why the station had not reported more fully from Tehran between 15 and 19 August. Sinclair is not a demonstrative person, but there was a definite glow emanating from him when Strang with apparent heartiness responded to the explanations, remarking that Roosevelt had done the only possible thing and that in matters of that sort decisions could only be made on the spot. As they came out of Strang's office, one of Sinclair's staff came up to him in great glee with a folder covered with red ribbons, sealing wax, and other *objets d'art*. Sinclair told Roosevelt that this represented approval of a project which they had been previously turned down by the Foreign Office and that this reversal of the Foreign Office was due to the success in Iran.

ON AUG. 19, 1953, MOSSADEQ TURNED HIMSELF IN and was put on trial by judges allied with the Shah. Mossadeq was sentenced to death for "trying to overthrow the monarchy," but his sentence was commuted and he was placed under house arrest in his village outside Tehran until his death in 1967. "My only crime," Mossadeq said during his trial, "is that I nationalized the oil industry and removed from this land the network of colonialism and the political and economic influence of the greatest empire on Earth."

10

WHAT WAS LEARNED
FROM THE OPERATION

TWO ELEMENTS LENDING SUPPORT to the operation seemed unable to meet the sudden demand for utmost speed and accomplishment. These were Communications and the Psychological Warfare (PW) Senior Staff. Many individual communications officers—at Headquarters, Nicosia, and Tehran—worked many extra hours and displayed commendable zeal and initiative in dealing with a great volume of traffic. Between 14 May and 1 September a total of 990 Ajax messages entered or left Headquarters. The unsatisfactory phase of communications was the three-way link between Headquarters, Nicosia, and Tehran by which MECA facilities were made available for almost simultaneous transmission from any one of the three stations named to the other two. Until near the end of the period of the operation, there was considerable delay in Tehran messages destined for Nicosia and for those in the opposite direction. It may also be suggested that transmission time was not rapid as had been hoped. Very few "operational immediate" messages were originated by any of the three stations, but when Tehran sent such a message it took from three to four hours to get to Headquarters measured from the time the enciphered message was filed for transmission until the deciphered message reached the branch desk.

In July support was sought from the PW Staff. Both the branch and higher levels were anxious to have certain items, including the texts of news articles, commentaries and editorials, appear in papers in this country. The texts themselves were prepared by NE/4 Branch on themes agreed upon by Headquarters and the station. It was planned to cable summaries of such planted material to the station for distribution to the friendly local press and, hence, to backstop the active propaganda campaign against Mossadeq. This support was not forthcoming. It appeared to the branch as if the staff lacked contacts capable of placing material so that the American publisher was unwitting as to its source, as well as being able to see that no changes in theme or emphasis were made. In contrast to this relatively ineffective venture, the Iran desk of the State Department was able to place a CIA study in *Newsweek*, using the normal channel of desk officer to journalist. Recognizing the fact that the Agency is not able to employ such a channel as just described, it does appear that some improvement of capabilities might be desirable. Either those contacts used to secure the unwitting publication of material should be expanded and improved, or else there should be a provision made for passing material directly to cleared editors and owners of press media.

Throughout the course of the operation, members of the Agency were in touch with members of SIS in Washington, Nicosia, London, and—incidentally—Cairo. In all but one of these places, we were on their home ground and hence, in a position to penetrate their organization, particularly with regard to building up personal histories of its personnel. The apparent fact that this organization was quite ready to act as the junior partner in this operation has been covered in an earlier paragraph, as has the indication that individual SIS officers made a definite effort to win the friendship and confidence of their contacts. The existence of friction between SIS headquarters and the station at Nicosia was also of interest to us. However, of greatest interest from an operational point of view was the very limited number of personnel engaged in Middle East operations. At Nicosia there were only two officers and two typists to deal both with Iran and with several other countries of the Middle East. At London headquarters no individual was exclusively concerned with Iran, and the one specialist in the field appeared to be spread out over the Middle and Far East. This shortage of personnel was directly reflected in a number of ways which seemed quite surprising at first glance. An example of this is the fact that the representative in Washington had to spend a good part of his time in enciphering and deciphering. The character of this limited personnel was also of interest for we were informed that all the old colonial hands and all the veterans of the India Office had been dispensed with. Certainly the two Nicosia officers who were dealing with the Agency were both young and had a very sound foundation. The one in charge has had six years in the country and is extremely fluent in the language, while the younger, still a probationer, also knows the language well.

Other lessons learned from the operation relate to Headquarters and station capacities for planning, and to the capabilities of the local agents to execute general and specific directives. First, we may make a brief critique of Headquarters planning.

As had been pointed out in some detail in earlier pages, the operational plan grew directly from a series of basic assumptions, established by CIA in collaboration with SIS. In briefest review, the principal assumptions were:

1. The Shah could be persuaded to take desired action if all-out pressure were applied.

2. Assurance that the Shah was behind him would both cause Zahedi to act and would win him the support of many officers in key positions.

3. Forced with a choice between following the orders of the Shah and those of Mossadeq, the rank and file of the army and its officers would obey the Shah.

The assumptions, whether presented as such within the operational plan, or discussed in some unwitting survey of the current situation, were challenged. The American Ambassador and the State Department desk officer for Iran, as well as the Chief of GTI [Greek, Turkish, and Iranian Affairs] office at State, insisted that assumption number one above was completely unsound. Ambassador Henderson stated that the premise that the Shah would cooperate actively was fallacious.

The station at one point expressed a similar opinion in these words: "it (is) unrealistic (to) expect Shah (to) sponsor a coup supported by army." The Office of Intelligence and Research of the State Department, in a special study, dated 29 July 1953 and entitled "Estimate of the likelihood and possible consequences of Mossadeq's removal as Prime Minister," indicated a positive belief that the opposition to Mossadeq was weak, lacked a plan, and was composed of heterogeneous elements incapable of unified action. How was it that the Headquarters planners could be so at odds with every other well informed opinion? This was because the plan had a necessity to avoid acceptance of the status quo and could take a bolder stand because it was based upon the principle of strong, positive action to make the assumptions come true. It should be noted that during the conversations at Beirut and in the later exchange of messages, representatives of the field station accepted the assumptions to which they had objected earlier. Thus, as the time for action approached, complete harmony prevailed.

Not only did the basic assumptions stand their test, but other factors of the plan which had been determined by a detailed estimate of the psychology of the Persians, as discussed at Nicosia and Beirut, worked out about as anticipated. Specifically, it had been realized that not all the Persians involved in the plan would take the action required of them, that even those who took it might not follow through exactly as required and, therefore, that the operational aspect of the plan called for repetitive efforts on the targets. This analysis was correct. That the initial military aspect went astray may be charged directly to the Persians who at the very end refused to continue to accept the guidance which the station felt was so essential.

With regard to the fact that the military aspect of the plan was balanced, or complemented, by action designed to result in publicly expressed hostility to the government of Mossadeq, it was in this field that those in charge of executing the plan had to deviate the most from its details. The plan placed emphasis upon a program for a massive *bast*, or political sanctuary movement, against the government; but it was found impossible to bring this into being because of the dissolution of the Majlis and because the most influential religious leaders were not willing to make the commitments required of them. This unwillingness of the leaders had been foreseen by the planners, but they had been assured by the principal agents of SIS that these leaders would take whatever action was required of them. Failing in this respect, public hostility was fanned in a number of other ways, some suggested by the station to its agents and others thought up by agents. This activity has been covered in the earlier pages dealing with events in Tehran, and here it is necessary to repeat only one conclusion concerning what was learned during the operation as to the influence of the press in Iran. It must be admitted that in the years and months working with a subsidized press and its venal (or patriotic) journalists in Tehran, the station was still not sure whether it was achieving results comparable to the sums so spent. In July and early August every segment of the press with which we or the United Kingdom had working relations went all out against Mossadeq. As judged by the public reactions on the days following 16 August, there can be no doubt whatsoever that this campaign had reached a very large audience and had directly influenced their thinking in a most positive way. A separate analysis of this press operation should be made to serve as basic guidance in mounting future campaigns.

The operation was a time of testing for the U.S. principal agents and for those of the station agents who were committed to the effort. All these agents did a superb job. It is easy to say that they did such a good job because they were not merely carrying out orders but were heart and soul in favor of the operation. This is true, but the fact must not be overlooked that in recruiting these individuals over a considerable period of time the station wittingly selected people whose basic ideologies were in accord with U.S. policy toward Iran and the USSR. This factor should not be overlooked in future recruitment in Iran. A word should be said about the fact that the high caliber of the agents was reflected in their performances. In one of the most critical periods station principal agents [REDACTED] were out of touch with the station, but on their own initiative took actions of just the type the station would have assigned to them.

The performance of the indigenous agents is just one factor in the demonstration of the values received from long-term station planning. Another such factor of real importance was the capability of the station to produce indigenous documents on short order, documents which stood serious scrutiny shortly after they had been manufactured. This program has long been under development.

The operation did reveal a need for the development of other long-term assets. Important in this field is the procurement of safehouses, at least two of which should be kept completely uncontaminated until time of real emergency. While the executors of the plan made brilliant use of the grounds of the Embassy and of houses occupied by U.S. personnel, this effort could have been nullified by a careful watch on the Embassy by agents of the government.

Among the other long-term assets which the station feels should be developed are independent printing and reproduction facilities. The station believes that these facilities should be within the Embassy. This matter is now under discussion as it would appear that the movement of supplies into the Embassy and the removal of the finished products for distribution would create a serious security problem.

The major role in the execution of the operational plan was assumed by U.S. assets. This does not mean, however, that the operation could have been carried through without the active cooperation of the United Kingdom and their assets. For one thing, it would have been impossible to get the Shah to move had he not been finally convinced that both the U.S. and the UK were ready to support him. For another, had not the UK assets been cut in on the operation, they would either have exposed whatever they learned about it to the government or tried actively to see that it failed. The lesson here is clear. As in the larger world picture, U.S.-UK interests and activities must be coordinated. A great deal is to be gained by direct coordination in special fields of activity once both parties have recognized that their aims are really identical.

A final subject of interest concerns the security problems connected with such an operation. From the moment the project got under way, the NEA Division made a serious effort to put special security measures into effect; within the NEA Division and even within the NE/4 Branch the rule of "need to know" came into effect. However, by the time the operation had been concluded, a considerable number of people—British and Americans—were aware of what was going on. From the viewpoint of NE/4 Branch, which has listed all the individuals whom it knows were aware of the project and its purpose, the number was excessive—it totaled 89. How many others were told by people without the NE/4 Branch being aware of this, there is no way of knowing. It is true that the knowledge that there was direct U.S.-UK collaboration on the project was kept to a more restricted number. It is, however, suggested that in the future when an operation of similar magnitude and sensitivity is contemplated a special security officer be brought into the operation at its inception and be given the responsibility for keeping track of exactly who knows what about the project.

ONE OF THE LAST PHOTOS OF MOSSADEQ was taken while he was serving out his life sentence under house arrest. The picture, which has never been published in the United States, clearly illustrates how the once spirited and fiery nationalist leader had become frail and tired as he lived out the rest of his life in obscurity.

APPENDICES

ON THE NIGHT OF THE COUP, the newspaper office of the Marxist political party, Tudeh, was set on fire by unknown individuals, though street gangs, on the payroll of the CIA and British intelligence, were widely suspected. The CIA engaged in rampant acts of terrorism that were falsely attributed to supporters of Mossadeq in order to discredit the nationalist leader in the eyes of Iranians. The CIA also significantly overstated Mossadeq's tolerance of Marxist groups in order to paint him as pro-Soviet at a time when the Cold War was in full swing.

APPENDIX A

Initial Operation Plan
for Ajax as Cabled
from Nicosia to Headquarters
1 June 1953

Summary of Preliminary Plan Prepared
By SIS and CIA Representatives in Cyprus

I. Preliminary Action

A. Interim Financing of Opposition

1. CIA will supply $35,000 to Zahedi
2. SIS will supply $25,000 to Zahedi
3. SIS indigenous channels in Iran will be used to supply above funds to Zahedi.
4. CIA will attempt to subsidize key military leaders if this [is] necessary.

B. Acquisition Shah Cooperation

1. Stage 1: Convince the Shah that UK and U.S. have joint aim and remove pathological fear of British intrigues against him.

a. Ambassador Henderson call on the Shah to assure him of

U.S.-UK common aid and British supporting him not Mossadeq.

b. Henderson to say to the Shah that special U.S. representative will soon be introduced to him for presentation joint U.S.-UK plan.

2. <u>Stage 2</u>: Special U.S. representative will visit the Shah and present following:

a. <u>Presentation to the Shah</u>

(1) Both governments consider oil question secondary.

(2) Major issue is to maintain independence [sic] Iran and keep from the Soviet orbit. To do this Mossadeq must be removed.

(3) Present dynasty best bulwark [for] national sovereignty.

(4) While Mossadeq in power no aid for Iran from United States.

(5) Mossadeq must go.

(6) U.S.-UK financial aid will be forthcoming to successor government.

(7) Acceptable oil settlement will be offered but successor government will not be rushed into it.

b. <u>Demands on the Shah</u>

(1) You must take leadership in overthrow [of] Mossadeq.

(2) If not, you bear responsibility for collapse of country.

(3) If not, Shah's dynasty will fall and U.S.-UK backing of you will cease.

(4) Who do you want to head successor government? (Try and maneuver Shah into naming Zahedi.)

(5) Warning [sic] not to discuss approach.

(6) Plan on operation with Zahedi will be discussed with you.

II. <u>Arrangement with Zahedi</u>

A. After agreement with Shah per above, inform Zahedi he [will be] chosen to head successor government with U.S.-UK support.

B. Agree on specific plan for action and timetable for action. There are two ways to put Zahedi in office.

1. Quasi-legally, whereby the Shah names Zahedi Prime Minister by royal *farman*.
2. Military coup.

Quasi-legal method to be tried first. If successful at least part of machinery for military coup will be brought into action. If it fails, military coup will follow in a matter of hours.

III. Relations with Majlis

Important for quasi-legal effort: To prepare for such effort deputies must be purchased.

A. Basic aim is to secure 41 votes against Mossadeq and assure quorum for quasi-legal move by being able to depend on 53 deputies in Majlis. (SIS considers [that] 20 deputies now not controlled must be purchased.)

B. Approach to deputies to be done by SIS indigenous agent group. CIA will backstop where necessary by [applying] pressures [sic] on Majlis deputies and will provide part of the funds.

IV. Relations with Religious Leaders

Religious leaders should:

A. Spread word of their disapproval [of Prime Minister] Mossadeq.

B. As required, stage political demonstrations under religious cover.

C. Reinforce backbone of the Shah.

D. Make strong assurances over radio and in mosques after coup that new government [is] faithful [to] Moslem principles. Possibly as *quid pro quo* prominent cleric [Ayatollah] Borujerdi would be offered ministry without portfolio or consider implementing neglected article [of Iranian] constitution providing body [of] five *mullas* (religious leaders) to pass on orthodoxy of legislation.

E. [REDACTED] should be encouraged to threaten direct action against pro-Mossadeq deputies.

V. <u>Relations with Bazaar</u>

Bazaar contacts to be used to spread anti-government rumors and possibly close bazaar as anti-government expression.

VI. <u>Tudeh</u>

Zahedi must expect violent reaction from Tudeh and be prepared to meet with superior violence.
A. Arrest at least 100 Party and Front Group leaders.
B. Seal off South Tehran to prevent influx [of] Tudeh demonstrations.
C. Via black [propaganda] leaflets, direct Tudeh members not to take any action.

VII. <u>Press and Propaganda Progress</u>

A. Prior [to] coup, intensify anti-Mossadeq propaganda.

B. Zahedi should quickly appoint effective chief of government press and propaganda who will:

1. Brief all foreign correspondents.
2. Release advance prepared U.S. and UK official statements.
3. Make maximum use Radio Tehran.

VIII. Relations with Tribes

A. Coup will provoke no action from Bakhtiari, Lurs, Kurds, Baluchi, Zolfaghari, Mamassani, Boer Ahmadi, and Khamseh tribal groups.

B. Major problem is neutralization of Qashqa'i tribal leaders.

IX. Mechanics of Quasi-Legal Overthrow

A. At this moment the view with most favor is the so-called [REDACTED] plan—whereby mass demonstrators [will] seek religious refuge in Majlis grounds. Elements available to religious leaders would be joined by those supplied by bazaar merchants, up to 4,000 supplied by SIS controlled group, and additional elements supplied through CIA.

B. Would be widely publicized that this refuge movement [was] on [the] basis [of] two grounds [of] popular dissatisfaction with Mossadeq government as follows:

1. Ground one that Mossadeq government [is] basically anti-religious as most clearly demonstrated [by] ties between Mossadeq and Tudeh; and Mossadeq and USSR. Just prior to movement CIA would give widest publicity to all fabricated documents proving secret agreement between Mossadeq and Tudeh.

2. Ground two that Mossadeq is leading the country into complete economic collapse through his unsympathetic dictatorship. Just prior to movement CIA would give widest publicity to the evidence of illegally issued paper money. CIA might have capability to print masses excellent imitation currency.

C. Religious refuge to take place at dawn of the coup day. Immediately followed by effort have Majlis pass a motion to censure the government. This is to be followed by the dismissal of Mossadeq and the appointment of Zahedi as successor. If successful, the coup would be completed by early afternoon. Failing success, the coup would be mounted later that evening.

THE FIGHT OVER IRAN'S OIL

CIA operative Dr. Donald Wilber, the author of this top-secret report, attempted to downplay the emphasis on controlling Iran's oil, but most historians today recognize that this was not the case. The following is an excerpt from a study written by the Iran Chamber Society, a non-profit foundation that acts as a clearinghouse for Iranian history and culture.

THE OPERATION, CODE-NAMED TP-AJAX, was the blueprint for a succession of CIA plots to foment coups and destabilize governments during the cold war—including the agency's successful coup in Guatemala in 1954 and the disastrous Cuban intervention known as the Bay of Pigs in 1961. In more than one instance, such operations led to the same kind of long-term animosity toward the United States that occurred in Iran.

The history says agency officers orchestrating the Iran coup worked directly with royalist Iranian military officers, handpicked the prime minister's replacement, sent a stream of envoys to bolster the shah's courage, directed a campaign of bombings by Iranians posing as members of the Communist Party, and planted articles and editorial cartoons in newspapers. . . .

The coup had its roots in a British showdown with Iran, restive under decades of near-colonial British domination. The prize was Iran's oil fields. Britain occupied Iran in World War II to protect a supply route to its ally, the Soviet Union, and to prevent the oil from falling into the hands of the Nazis—ousting the shah's father, whom it regarded as unmanageable. It retained control over Iran's oil after the war through the Anglo-Iranian Oil Company. In 1951, Iran's Parliament voted to nationalize the oil industry, and legislators backing the law elected its leading advocate, Dr. Mossadeq, as prime minister. Britain responded with threats and sanctions. . . .

GENERAL H. NORMAN SCHWARZKOPF, the father of the now-famous General Schwarzkopf of Iraq War I, was picked by the CIA to talk the Shah into participating in the Anglo-American coup d'etat. Schwarzkopf was brought in because of his long-time relationship with Iran's royal family. He was tasked with convincing the Shah's sister—and likewise the Shah himself—that Iran's relations with the West depended on the Shah seizing power and that oil was not the priority of the Americans and the British.

APPENDIX B

London Draft
Of the Ajax
Operational Plan

I. INTRODUCTION

The policy of both the U.S. and UK governments requires replacement of Mossadeq as the alternative to certain economic collapse in Iran and the eventual loss of the area to the Soviet orbit. Only through a planned and controlled replacement can the integrity and independence of the country be ensured.

General Zahedi is the only figure in Iran currently capable of heading a new government who could be relied upon to repress Soviet-Communist penetration and carry out basic reforms.

The plan which follows is comprised of three successive stages. The first two stages precede action of a military nature. They include the present preliminary support period and the mass propaganda campaign. (See paragraphs below.) These stages will be of real value to the mutual interests of U.S. and UK even if final military action is not carried out in that they will make the position of Mossadeq increasingly vulnerable and unsteady.

The total estimated expenditure required to implement this plan will be the equivalent of $285,000 of which $147,000 will be provided by the U.S. Service and $137,500 by the UK Service.

II. OPERATIONAL PLAN

A. Preliminary Support of Opposition to Mossadeq Government

For a period of several months both the U.S. field station and the British group (the Rashidian brothers) have been in close touch with Zahedi. The British group has supplied the equivalent of $50,000 (four to five million rials) for this support.

During this preliminary period beginning 1 June 1953, and for an estimated two months maximum thereafter, the United States will provide $35,000 and the United Kingdom the equivalent of $25,000. Initial payments under this allocation have already been made by the U.S. field station.

British funds will continue to be paid through present channels for purposes as directed by the UK or by the U.S. field station on UK behalf.

U.S. funds are to be distributed through direct U.S. fields station contracts for the specific purpose of extending and strengthening military and political contacts of Zahedi.

Early in this period Zahedi will be made fully aware of this dual support and of the joint intention that it should lead to even more concrete support.

During this period the impression will continue to be given in the circle of Zahedi's contacts that the Shah is supporting him by the provision of funds.

The coordination of UK-U.S. field station activity on the developing plan will be achieved through direct contact between U.S. field personnel and the British group with the former acting on behalf of the United Kingdom by relaying instructions and acting as a secure communication link, to augment that already existing.

Appropriate steps will be taken to ensure that overt U.S. policy will conform as closely as possible with the purpose of this plan.

B. Role of the Shah as Focal Point of Opposition

This plan is based on the assumption that the cooperation of the Shah will be obtained. Such cooperation will give a military coup the best chance of success. However, it also envisages the same type of operation through the involuntary involvement of the Shah in this plan.

To play his role the Shah requires special preparation. By nature a creature of indecision, beset by formless doubts and fears, he must be induced to play his role, and this role must require a minimum of affirmative action and cover as brief a period as possible.

We consider Princess Ashraf, his forceful and scheming twin sister, to be the person most likely to be able to induce the Shah to play his role.

We are certain that Ashraf will eagerly cooperate to bring about the fall of Mossadeq. Therefore, Ashraf must be approached at her present location, briefed on the task and sent back to Iran. Contact will have to be maintained between Ashraf and the U.S. field situation.

The role of the Shah is to be played in three stages, and Ashraf will be preparing him in advance for each successive stage.

The first stage will be to convince the Shah that the United States and the United Kingdom have a joint aim in Iran, and at the same time to remove his pathological fear of the "hidden UK hand"; the second stage will be to inform him in specific terms of what the immediate future holds for him. The third stage will be to obtain specific items from him. These stages are detailed below:

1. First Stage:

With prior advice from Princess Ashraf, the leader of the British group will visit the Shah to assure him that the United States and the United Kingdom have common aims towards Iran, and that both want to support him to the utmost in opposing Mossadeq. The leader of the British group will say that he is in a position to prove that the British are supporting the Shah and that he, the leader, is authorized to speak for the United Kingdom by stating that any key phrases selected by the Shah out of several proposed will be given on successive dates in the Persian language broadcasts over the BBC.

PRINCESS ASHRAF PAHLAVI, the twin sister of the Shah, was utilized by U.S. intelligence to convince Mohammad Reza Pahlavi to come back to Iran and take power in 1953. Ashraf has been viewed by some historians as instrumental in the coup because without her help, it is doubtful as to whether the Shah would have seized power. For her own efforts, Ashraf received $10,000 and a mink coat from the CIA.

2. <u>Second Stage:</u>

With advance warning from Princess Ashraf, General Schwarzkopf (former head of the U.S. Military Mission to the Iranian Gendarmerie) is introduced as the U.S. special representative. This representative is already well known to and admired by the Shah as a result of his successful tour of duty in Iran some years ago.

His remarks to the Shah will comprise two parts.

The first part covers the following points:

a. Both governments consider the oil issue of secondary importance at this time, since the major is the resolve for both governments to maintain the independence of Iran. Both governments are now determined to help the Iranians to help themselves to keep their country from falling into Soviet hands. If Mossadeq remains in power economic collapse is certain, and since Mossadeq is permitting extensive Communist penetration, the economic collapse would be followed by a Communist takeover of the country.

b. Both governments feel that the continued existence of the Pahlavi dynasty should be the best bulwark of national sovereignty.

c. As long as Mossadeq is in power the country will get no new financial aid from the United States and indeed present aid may be slashed.

d. Mossadeq must go.

e. His successor will have the strong support of both governments through the same forces that bring him into power.

f. An acceptable oil settlement will be offered, but there is no intention of either rushing this issue or of forcing it on the country.

The second part will cover the following points:

a. The Shah is now, and inevitably will remain, the focal point of all forces opposing Mossadeq.

b. If the Shah fails to go along with these forces he will be solely responsible for the collapse of the country and its loss of independence.

c. If the Shah fails to go along, his dynasty is bound to come to an end soon. In spite of the Shah's previous misconceptions, the United States and the United Kingdom have been and are supporting him, but if the Shah fails now, this support will be withdrawn. The representative will discuss the implications of this.

d. The Shah has stated that Zahedi is acceptable to him as his successor to Mossadeq. Furthermore, the Shah has asked that funds for Zahedi's support given by the United States and United Kingdom governments should be given out in his name.

e. The U.S. and UK governments agree fully that Zahedi is the only effective candidate. Zahedi will be ready to take over in the near future, aided in every way to achieve success by the United States and United Kingdom. The Shah will be kept fully informed of Zahedi's plans and a minimum of action will be required from him. As soon as possible after the visit of the U.S. representative to the Shah, the leader of the British group will make a visit of identical type to reinforce the above estimates.

3. Third Stage:

This stage will be the sole responsibility of Princess Ashraf. Immediately following the visits as described above, and while the Shah is still under their effects, Princess Ashraf will obtain his signature on three documents. The first of these documents will be dated, the second and the third undated.

They will be:

a. An open letter calling on all loyal officers to cooperate with the bearer of the letter in any efforts he feels are necessary to reestablish the prestige of the Army, to restore their own self respect and to show their devotion to the Shah and country.

b. A royal decree naming Zahedi as Chief of Staff.

c. A royal decree appealing to all ranks of the Army, to carry out faithfully the orders of the Chief of Staff whom the Shah has named.

These documents will be then taken out of the palace at once; the first to be delivered to Zahedi and the other two to be held by the U.S. station [for] time of need.

Following the effort required of him to produce these documents the Shah may be in a period of elation for some time. Sooner or later he will begin to brood and to doubt, and at this time he must be removed from the capital to make some kind of tour. Preferably he would make a religious retreat to the Meshed Shrine [in the holy city of Meshed, north of Tehran]. He would remain at this shrine until after Zahedi obtains control and would return to the capital only to give his official approval to the new Prime Minister.

C. Arrangement with Zahedi

Continuing contacts by U.S. personnel and British agents with Zahedi or his representatives have helped to bring into increasingly clear focus the picture of his tentative plans and of those elements from which he expects support. This material and related intelligence reports have been used in the preparation of later paragraphs which follow under the subtitle "Organization to Mount Coup," with its supporting material in the annexes.

Following the phased contacts with the Shah as given above, both the United States and the United Kingdom will inform Zahedi directly that they have secured a firm commitment from the Shah on his behalf and that the time has come to move to a detailed plan of action.

General Zahedi will be given the letter signed by the Shah calling on all loyal officers to cooperate with the bearer. He will be instructed to recruit, with the aid of this letter, military aides. Zahedi will also be shown the U.S.-UK proposal for action entitled "Organization to Overthrow Mossadeq." It will be discussed with Zahedi who will have the opportunity to amend or modify this proposal should this be necessary to meet his desires and capabilities. It will be pointed out to Zahedi that the plan provides for full U.S.-UK coordinated covert support prior to the time of the coup. Every element of the potential opposition to Mossadeq will be mustered so that on coup day it may be possible to overthrow the Mossadeq government by legal means. It will be pointed out to Zahedi that the future character and reputation of the successor government would be better if military action could be limited to assuring control of the city coincident with this legal success.

However, should the Shah fail to go along with the U.S. representative or fail to produce the documents for General Zahedi, Zahedi would be informed that the United States and United Kingdom would be ready to go ahead without the Shah's active cooperation if Zahedi agrees. We would continue to make every effort to associate the Shah with the undertaking involuntarily and so hope to achieve the same result as if he had actively participated.

D. Organization to Mount Overthrow

The material which follows under this heading is that which is to be presented to Zahedi by the U.S. field station for the purpose of discussion and modification.

Under the headings which follow, elements of existing or potential are assigned their specific roles. This approach omits any consideration of the strengths of the pro-Mossadeq forces.

1. Organization to Mount Coup

a. Military secretariat. This secretariat, headed by an officer named Zahedi but acceptable to the United States and United Kingdom will be composed of a very limited number of capable senior officers. This secretariat will be in contact with the U.S. field station which will hand over a preliminary staff plan jointly prepared by the United States and the United Kingdom for securing Tehran. A sum equivalent to $75,000 will be required for the military secretariat to carry out its functions.

b. Duties of the secretariat. Its most urgent duty will be the selection of key officers in Tehran who can be counted upon or won over for action against the Mossadeq government. For security reasons, such officers will be informed of their own actual role at the latest possible date.

This secretariat will make a detailed examination of the U.S. and the UK staff plan with the special attention to every action to be carried out on coup day. Some of these actions will be immediate seizures of general staff headquarters, army radio station, Radio Tehran, the houses of Mossadeq and his entourage, police and gendarmerie headquarters, post and telegraph offices, telephone exchange, the Majlis and its printing press, and the

National Bank and its printing press. Arrests will include the key figures of the Mossadeq government, key army officers cooperating with Mossadeq, and selected newspaper editors.

Special attention will also be given to preparing measures to be taken against the Tudeh Party. Zahedi must expect a violent reaction from the Tudeh Party, and must be fully prepared to meet it with superior violence. There is no possibility of neutralizing the party until after the Mossadeq government has been replaced. However, there will be a breathing spell of several hours after the change of government before the Tudeh Party will be able to get out on the streets in force. At the time of the coup at least 100 party and front group leaders and journalist must be arrested: these names will come from a list of approximately 80 such leaders recently prepared by the United Kingdom, plus U.S. station additions, plus Zahedi's own additions. Control of the Tehran streets will prevent the massing of Tudeh or other mob elements. Mass distribution of black [propaganda] pamphlets, notionally issued by the Central Committee of the Party, will be made with the purpose of confusing Tudeh members and of preventing them from assembling in an effective manner. It may be possible for the United States to supply by air in advance stocks of tear gas, indelible ink, or other materials suitable for the control of mobs. Local air force planes may drop warnings to the public to stay off the streets or take the consequences.

c. Action on coup day. This action will follow basically similar lines although it may be carried out relative to as many as three different situations. These three situations are:

Situation A: The climax of a massive religious protest against the Mossadeq government which is followed immediately by military action.

Situation B: The moment when the Shah is being forced by Mossadeq to leave the country. This action by Mossadeq will have resulted from either the growing strength of the opposition as knowingly led by the Shah or because of its growing strength with the Shah as its involuntary figurehead.

Situation C: The moment when Mossadeq attempts to present

his resignation, such an action might result from his real concern over the growing strength of the opposition and might take the form, on past showing, or calling on the Shah for personal support. Failing to win the support of the Shah he might summon the mobs into the streets.

Action to be taken with regard to Situation A will be as follows:

At the climax of Situation A, Zahedi will assume office as Chief of the General Staff by a limited military action against the headquarters of the general staff. He will at once name the selected person as his deputy, and the arrests of Mossadeq and the others will be made at once. The Majlis will be called into session and the opposition will attempt to pass a vote of censure against Mossadeq and will follow this with a vote of support for Zahedi. However, with or without the possession of a royal decree naming him as prime minister, Zahedi will take over the government and will execute the various requirements of coup day (see above). Once he has firmly established his control, he will have no trouble in obtaining the formal vote of support from the Majlis. Only then will the Shah return to Tehran.

Action to be taken with regard to Situations B and C will be as follows:

The only changes in plan will be the necessary advancement of the timetable for coup day to the day of actual crisis and the necessity of putting all the military aspects of the coup machinery into operation at once.

2. Organization to Create Maximum Public Opposition to Mossadeq Prior to the Coup

a. General Progress. The purpose will be to create, extend, and enhance public hostility and distrust and fear of Mossadeq and his government. A sum equivalent to $150,000 will be budgeted for this program. This will be a phased operation, with the phases as follows:

Phase 1. This is the current preliminary support stage wherein the receipt of U.S. and UK funds permits Zahedi to win additional friends and to influence key people.

Phase 2. A massive propaganda campaign against Mossadeq and his government but with Mossadeq himself as the principal target. This will begin only a week or two before the climax of Situation A so as not to offer too much time for a sharp reaction by Mossadeq and so that the impact will not be dispersed by being long and drawn out.

Phase 3. This is Situation A, which is described in full in a following paragraph.

b. Duties of Specific Elements

1. Press and publicity. In the preliminary support period the British group will continue to use its numerous smaller papers to push an anti-Mossadeq line. At Headquarters and at the field station U.S. personnel will draft and put into Persian the texts for articles, broadsheets and pamphlets, some pro-Shah and some anti-Mossadeq. The material designed to discredit Mossadeq will hammer the following themes.

a. Mossadeq favors the Tudeh Party and the USSR. (This will be supported by black documents.)

b. Mossadeq is an enemy of Islam since he associates with the Tudeh and advances their aims.

c. Mossadeq is deliberately destroying the morale of the Army and its ability to maintain order.

d. Mossadeq is deliberately fostering the growth of regional separatist elements through his removal of Army control over tribal areas. One of the aims of the removal of control by the Army is to make it easier for the Soviets to take over the Northern Provinces.

e. Mossadeq is deliberately leading the country into economic collapse.

f. Mossadeq has been corrupted by power to such an extent that no trace is left of the fine man of earlier years, and he now has all the repressive instincts of [a] dictator.

g. Consistent with these themes will be the persistent slant that Mossadeq has been the unwitting victim of his unscrupulous, personally ambitious advisors.

It is considered essential that Zahedi make an early choice of the man who will be his director of press and propaganda and who may be deputy prime minister as well. The U.S. field station will obtain from Zahedi the name of the man he has in mind who must be acceptable to the United States and the United Kingdom. One or two weeks before the date set for Situation A, the intensive propaganda effort will begin. The details relative to the execution of this campaign will be the primary responsibility of the U.S. field station.

Immediately after the change of government, Zahedi's director of press and propaganda must be prepared to:

a. Make maximum use of Radio Tehran.

b. Through Radio Tehran, posters, special news sheets, etc, spread the progress of broadcast appeal presented in simplest terms, such as immediate slashes in living costs, increased pay for government officials and Army personnel, etc.

c. Give maximum local publicity to U.S. and UK statements which will have been prepared in advance.

d. Brief all foreign correspondents.

(2) The Majlis. If the Majlis is in session at the time of the coup, an effort will be made to have the change of government formalized. If it is not in session it will be called into session by one of its elected officers who will have to be a member of the anti-Mossadeq opposition.

To prepare for the change of government, a number of the deputies will be approached and purchased. It is yet to be decided whether the purchases are to be made by the British group or directly by Zahedi himself who, as long as he enjoys the sanctuary of the Majlis building, is in excellent position to achieve such an aim. Following the receipt from one or both of the above elements of a list of deputies with the amounts required for the purchase of each one, a special funding operation will be established within the framework of the joint authorization for the execution of this plan. The U.S. field station will also employ various agents and contacts to support this operation.

Its basic aim will be to secure a majority plus one vote against Mossadeq as required in Situation A. At the present time it is estimated that at least 30 deputies are prepared to vote against Mossadeq if they think there is a good chance that they will be in a majority. It is to be noted that all Majlis elected members would not normally be present at any one session. However, it will also be necessary to attempt to ensure that a quorum can be maintained in the Majlis at the moment when the anti-Mossadeq vote is to be taken. The minimum quorum requirement is that two-thirds of the deputies present in Tehran must be in the Chamber before a vote can be taken. Thus an effort will be made to purchase additional deputies solely to have them remain in the Chamber to ensure the quorum and not for the more sensitive role of voting against Mossadeq.

(3) Political elements other than the Tudeh.

Political parties or groups now opposed to Mossadeq will play only a very minor role in this campaign. Such parties as the Toilers Party, the Sumka and sections of the Pan-Iranists could supply only limited and probably ineffectual street gangs. The Toilers Party will, however, play a fairly important role in the publicity described above.

It is to be noted that while these parties command only ineffectual street gangs, the British group can muster up to approximately 3,000 street activists to be committed in Situation A.

(4) Religious leaders. It is our belief that nearly all the important religious leaders with large followings are firmly opposed to Mossadeq. Both the U.S. field station and the British group have firm contacts with such leaders. The pro-Zahedi capabilities in this field are very great.

These leaders include such assorted and sometimes inimical elements as the non-political leaders [REDACTED] and [[REDACTED], as well as [[REDACTED] and [[REDACTED] and his terrorist gang, [[REDACTED]. During the period of intensive anti-Mossadeq publicity before coup day the leaders and their henchmen will:

(a) Spread word of their disapproval of Mossadeq.

(b) Give open support to the symbol of the throne and give

moral backing to the Shah through direct contact with him at the shrine.

(c) As required, stage small pro-religious anti-Mossadeq demonstrations in widely scattered sections of Tehran.

(d) The terrorist group [sic] to threaten that they are ready to take direct action against pro-Mossadeq deputies and members of Mossadeq's entourage and government.

(e) Ensure full participation of themselves and followers in Situation A.

(f) After the change of government, give the strongest assurances over Radio Tehran and in the mosques that the new government is faithful to religious principles.

(5) <u>Bazaar Merchants</u>. These are defined as a relatively small number of long established prominent merchants with a semi-religious outlook and with strong influence over the lower social orders in the bazaar section. Contacts with these merchants exist both through the British group and through the U.S. field station.

These merchants are anti-Mossadeq because the government harms them directly through the stagnation of business, the cutting off of imports, the strenuous collection of taxes, and the general tightness of money.

In the period of intensive publicity preceding Situation A, these merchants will be used to:

(a) Spread anti-Government rumors in the bazaar.

(b) Stage limited protests in the south of Tehran against the economic policies of the Mossadeq government. Then, at the time of Situation A, they will:

(c) Close all or part of the bazaar.

(c) <u>Final Action Immediately Preceding the Coup</u>. As noted above, the military action can result from Situation A, B, and C. However, the pre-coup activities of the organization as described above will be primarily for the purpose of creating Situation A which is described below.

(1) On the appointed day, staged attacks will be made against respected religious leaders in Tehran.

(2) Other religious leaders will at once say that these attacks were ordered by Mossadeq as his reaction to the disfavor in which his government is held by the religious leaders of the entire country.

(3) A number of the more important leaders will at once take sanctuary in the Majlis grounds.

(4) At this time, these religious leaders will release statements through their followers denouncing in the strongest terms the anti-religious attitudes and behavior of Mossadeq.

(5) At the same time as 2.b. (4 d) above, the fullest publicity will be given to the U.S. station fabricated documents which prove and record in detail a secret agreement between Mossadeq and the Tudeh, with the latter promising to use all their force in support of Mossadeq and against the religious leaders, the army, and the police.

(6) Simultaneously, these leaders will call on their followers to take sanctuary all over Tehran in mosques, telegraphs and post offices, banks, etc. The British group and the U.S. station will supply all the demonstrators they can to swell their ranks, and at the same time the merchants will attempt to close the bazaar. (this mass sanctuary is designed to interrupt all normal life and activity in the city and to illustrate dramatically the extent of popular dis-satisfaction with the government. It is the local version of passive resistance and by long established tradition the military and police are unable to take action against people who take sanctuary.)

(7) In the presence of this increasingly hostile and abnormal atmosphere, Zahedi will take over as chief of staff and make those arrests which are an essential part of the military phase of the coup.

(8) Just after Zahedi moves, the Majlis will be called into session to formalize the change of government and complete the coup.

II. <u>ESTIMATE OF CHANCES OF SUCCESS OF OPERATIONAL PLAN</u>

The preceding material represents a Western-type plan offered for execution by Orientals. However, It was drafted by authors with an intensive knowledge of the country and its people who endeavored to examine and evaluate all the details from the Iranian point of view. Given the recognized incapacity of Iranians to plan or act in a thoroughly logical manner, we would never expect such a plan to be re-studied and executed in the local atmosphere like a Western staff operation.

However, we feel that the plan is broad enough and sufficiently comprehensive to offer a reasonable chance of success even if not carried out 100 percent.

Security among all local elements involved is a serious weakness inherent in the Persian character. We must be aware of the fact that security breaches might lead to repressive measures by Mossadeq.

No precedent for this proposed operation exists in Iran in recent years. The Reza Hah coup was of an entirely different nature. Recent coups in other Near Eastern countries were far easier to carry out since they were not complicated by a large pro-Communist opposition or hampered by the presence of a head of government having powerful popular following.

Prior to an estimate of the chances of success, the following points in connection with the general concept of the coup are vital:

A. The failure of the coup would result in:

1. A strong tide of government-directed hostility toward the United States and the possibility of the United States being expelled from Iran.

2. Loss to the United Kingdom only of operational machinery represented by the group which is intended mainly for the overthrow of Mossadeq.

B. Should the coup be attempted and fail, but the United States is not expelled from Iran and should Mossadeq then fall at a subsequent date, neither the United States nor the United Kingdom would be in a position to take advantage of that opportunity since the British group and certain U.S. assets may be destroyed by the failure of the coup.

C. If the coup is not undertaken, the United States still stands to be expelled from Iran as the certain economic collapse under the present Mossadeq government would probably be accompanied by internal chaos and a subsequent takeover by the Tudeh under USSR direction.

D. If the coup plan is rejected at this time, then another plan should be prepared against the time of economic collapse and internal chaos.

[III.] <u>Conclusion</u>: Subject to the Shah's support, Zahedi's acceptance of the basic features of this plan, our approval of his modifications, and to our feeling certain that he will act according to an established timetable, the authors of this plan believe that the coup will succeed.

IV. <u>ANNEXES</u>
These proposed annexes are not included in this draft as they must be based upon a great mass intelligence and information which is still being specifically collected for this purpose.

Annexes would include very detailed listings of all support available or probably available to Zahedi such as names and positions of army officers backing him, critical examination of the position of army officers backing him, critical examination of the position of the Majlis deputies, appraisal of size and cohesion of religious leaders supporting Zahedi, the proposed cabinet of Zahedi, etc.

ABOVE: QUEEN ELIZABETH II of England and Shah Mohammad Reza Pahlavi in the early 1960s. The overthrow of Mossadeq ended the fledgling nationalist era for Iran, heralding in a repressive monarchy highlighted by the brutal domestic intelligence organization, Savak, with the help of the CIA and the Israelis. Savak was tasked with monitoring and detaining political dissidents opposed to Iran's monarchy. Noted for its arbitrary detentions and cruel torture, the group operated with impunity up until the Iranian revolution and the Shah's departure in 1979.

APPENDIX C

Foreign Office Memorandum
of 23 July 1953 from
British Ambassador Makins to
Assistant Under Secretary of State Smith

"Her Majesty's Government have noted the State Department's view as got out in a report on the conversation between Mr. Byroads and Mr. Bealey on 7 July, and have much sympathy for him.

"The overriding consideration is that the whole question of compensation must be left to the impartial arbitration of an international tribunal. Furthermore the term[s] of any future arrangements must be such as not to appear to provide a reward for the tearing up of contractual obligations or to disturb the pattern of world oil prices. Subject to this Her Majesty's Government are prepared to go to the utmost to help . . . with the problem of presenting an agreement to the public locally. They are also convinced that the Company, who have not been consulted, will adopt a generous attitude as regards methods and duration of payments as regards any compensation awarded to them.

"The answers therefore to the specific questions raised in the report from Washington Embassy are as follows:

"(a) The United Kingdom can do without this oil, although it would be an advantage to have it flowing into its traditional markets [the UK] once more. Her Majesty's Government are, however, anxious to dispose of the dispute which poison[s] their relations with the country concerned and is a disturbing element in the area as a whole. They would therefore 'be ready to cooperate' with a new government in trying to reach an agreement, provided that the principles referred to in paragraph 2 above are safeguarded.

"(b) Her Majesty's Government take the wording of the plan to mean that the initiative would be left to the future Prime Minister both as to the priority of an oil agreement in relation to his general programme and as to the nature of it. They hope he would agree to look at the February proposals, and they would of course 'help him in regards to the presentation of the agreement.' If he had any alternative proposals, Her Majesty's Government would consider them with equal sympathy, subject always to the principles mentioned above being safeguarded."

Britain's Meddling in Iran

Britain has long been involved in meddling in Persian affairs. Over the course of the 19th century, the importance of Persia grew in direct proportion to the ambitions of the British Empire. Britain regarded Persia, with its key, central location, as the logical extension of its Indian possessions.

In the face of a wave of anti-imperialist sentiment, Britain used a policy of "divide and rule," aimed at destroying the central government's authority by encouraging and arming tribal chiefs and warlords to resist any attempt by the shahs to assert authority over southern Persia.

The furor of the Persian people culminated in the Constitutional Revolution of 1906-1907, a response to the impotency of the Iranian autocracy in the face of the escalating imperial encroachments of Britain, which overthrew the monarchy.

The constitutionalists' quest to transform Persia into a modern nation-state was crushed by the signing of the Anglo-Russian Agreement of 1907. The bilateral accord (Iranians had no say in it) split the nation into three sections: two "spheres of influence" divided by a central "neutral zone," over which the Iranian parliament, or Majlis, nominally retained sovereignty. The pact granted the agents of either empire exclusive control over the disposition of the natural resources contained within their respective "sphere."

The geo-strategic importance of Persia to the British Empire escalated in 1908, with the discovery of vast petroleum deposits within the British sphere of influence. An infusion of materiel from Britain allowed the Iranian army, under Reza Mizra Khan's personal command, to successfully invade and occupy the former Russian sphere of influence. Backed by the British, Reza Khan dropped all pretense of constitutional rule and had himself crowned shah of Iran on December 13, 1925, establishing the Pahlavi dynasty. As everyone knows, the monarchy was ousted again, this time by the mullahs, in recent history, so that Iran is now an Islamic republic.

For Iranians, democracy is not a new idea but an ongoing struggle. For a century, this Middle East Muslim country has sought democracy, only to see its efforts twice stamped out by Western powers. The time has come for Britain, and the West in general, to stop meddling in the affairs of Iran.

THE COUP TAKES SHAPE. Above, at the height of the coup d'etat, chaos engulfed Tehran as protesters, many of whom were on the payroll of CIA and British agents, ran throughout the streets, looting and setting fire to buildings. Above, pro-Shah forces, guarded by club-wielding thugs, parade a tank through the streets of Tehran, announcing the return of the Shah.

APPENDIX D

Report on Military Planning
Aspect of Ajax

Military Aspects Operation Ajax

In early summer 1953 [George] Carroll was assigned the task of planning military aspects of Ajax. Several assumptions first had to be taken into account:

A. Operation would be joint operation with SIS.

B. Operation would rely heavily upon military willingness to fight for Shah.

C. Armed forces in Iran under Mossadeq very strongly led by pro-Mossadeq officers.

D. Operational assets within armed forces controlled by SIS or CIA were not at the outset capable of executing the military objectives of Ajax.

Planning tasks which had to be accomplished:

E. Detailed study of the leading military personalities in Iran.

F. Detailed study of order of battle of the Iranian army with emphasis on the Tehran garrison.

G. Detailed military study of communications, supply dumps, ammunition depots, command structure Iranian armed forces, time and distance factors within Tehran and throughout Iran, including road and rail nets.

H. Detailed [military study of] assets possessed by SIS.

I. Operational assets to be developed by CIA; almost no military assets were then under CIA control.

George Carroll in Washington began a staff study preliminary to drafting a military plan. Persons who were particularly helpful in the preparation of this study were Jerome F. Begert, Willima Fowlkes, Jr., Eugene E. Cilsdorf, Elizabeth E. McNeill, Betty J. Caldwell, and Arthur W. Dubois. This group constituted a branch task force.

Throughout the summer cables were exchanged with the Tehran Station in an effort to procure the latest information on the order of battle of Iranian armed forces. The Iranian desk, G-2, Pentagon, was queried in an effort to obtain whatever information they could get which might help accomplish the above tasks. Information available in G-2 was almost non-existent. Biographical information on leading Army figures was extremely scanty. G-2 did not possess a tactical map showing the military situation in the city of Tehran. It must also be admitted that CIA too was unprepared for this type of operational plan and a heavy burden had to be laid upon the field at a time when the Tehran Station was already occupied with the opening phases of Ajax.

The primary difficulty in staff planning at this time was the fact that neither the field nor headquarters possessed detailed information on military figures in Iran.

CIA had heretofore never placed particular emphasis on that type of operational reporting, and we learned as the days went by how extremely important, indeed vital, that type of reporting is.

Throughout the month of June, the branch task force gradually was supplied information from the field which made it possible to begin thinking about the use of the forces within the Tehran garrison. The field reported that Tehran was garrisoned by five brigades, three infantry mountain brigades, and two armored brigades. In addition, four other military forces existed: the Gendarmerie, the police, the armed customs guard, and the forces under the military governor. It was also learned that the young Chief of Staff, Brigadier General Taghi Riahi, and his staff had been drawn primarily from members of the pro-Mossadeq Iran Party. It had to be assumed that the chief of staff and officers within all sections of his staff were under control of Mossadeq. It has also to be assumed that at least three out of five of the brigade commanders in Tehran were completely under General Riahi's control. Those assumptions proved to be correct. SIS reported that Colonel [Ashrafi, military governor of Tehran and commanding officer of the Third Mountain Brigade,] could be relied upon; this later turned out to be incorrect but for staff planning purposes in June it had to be assumed correct. It was disappointing to learn that Major General Zahedi, Prime Minister designate under Ajax, possessed almost no military assets. General Zahedi, therefore, could not be relied upon to execute his own staff plan. In the early part of July, the branch task force was able to draw up a plan designed to neutralize the Tehran garrison and to isolate all other brigades in Iran. It appeared at that time that only a very small force could be relied upon by CIA, primarily the Third Mountain Brigade in Tehran. Therefore, our first staff plan was based upon the use of the Third Mountain Brigade for the capture and arrest of the officers assigned to the Chief of Staff, as well as the arrest and neutralization of all other forces in the city of Tehran.

Because of the fact that CIA did not possess any military assets capable at that time of helping Ajax, it was suggested that Station agent Colonel [Aban Farzanegan] be given special training. [Farzanegan] was trained in a safehouse in Washington with the assistance of instructors from the training division. [Farzanegan] had no idea what lay before him. He had never previously participated in any military action, although he had been superbly trained [in logistics in the Command and General Staff School at Ft. Leavenworth. Further, he had been assistant military attache for Iran in Washington for several years, and] before that had been the [Iranian liaison officer to the United States Military Assistance Advisory Group in Tehran. He, therefore, had a good grasp of American army methods. He was a Signal Corps officer by profession.] Because of the extreme sensitivity of Ajax, [Farzanegan] was given the lie detector test. In early July, [Farzanegan] was directed to go to Tehran and to renew all of his old contacts within the Iranian army.

In June, Carroll was assigned TDY [temporary duty] to Cyprus to work with Donald Wilber, NEA Planning Officer, and SIS. Carroll concentrated on military planning aspects with SIS, and ascertained the extent to which SIS could control Iran military assets. Headquarters was extremely concerned because the plan assumed that the Shah would sign a *farman* dismissing Mossadeq without being certain that his army officers and men were well organized enough to force Mossadeq from office in the event Mossadeq did not obey the *farman*, since CIA and SIS did not possess military assets capable of being organized into an effective fighting force and it was feared that the development of new military assets and their organization into a fighting force could not be accomplished in time.

SIS in Cyprus stated that it did have several important friends among the military, but the only officer among their friends then in a position to be of assistance to us was Colonel [Ashrafi.] SIS agreed that our preliminary military plan must be based on the assumption that Colonel [Ashrafi] would cooperate. Military Planner Carroll doubted whether one brigade out of five would be sufficient to overthrow Mossadeq and stated frankly that our military plan must be viewed as extremely tentative; he also stated that he hoped upon arrival in Tehran to find other assets in addition to Colonel [Ashrafi.] From the military point of view the discussions in Cyprus were extremely disappointing because they made it clear that they wanted to accomplish much but had very little with which to accomplish it. It also made it clear that Carroll and Colonel [Farzanegan] should arrive in Tehran as soon as possible where the military plan would of necessity have to be completed.

On 15 July Carroll left for London where SIS studied the military plan for two days and approved it with little comment. They agreed that, if Ajax were to succeed, CIA must start from scratch and work quickly to find powerful friends among Iranian Army troop commanders. In London, Carroll with Major Keen and two other British Army officers on duty with SIS, went over two military plans which had been drawn by the branch task force.

Both of our military plans used the same arrest lists for military and civilian persons in Tehran. These lists were compiled as a result of a long study of pro-Mossadeq Iranians, and later proved to be at least 90 percent correct. The British approved the arrest lists after their CE [counter-espionage] expert and their biographical section studied them. A third arrest list, the Tudeh Arrest List, was studied very carefully by SIS Tudeh Party experts and was approved without addition. It would seem that our appraisal of Iranians must have been based upon approximately the same information.

While these arrest lists were farmed out to SIS experts, Carroll sat down to study the two military plans with Major Keen and with the British major. The first plan was based upon the assumption that [Colonel Ashrafi] was a controlled British agent [and that his Third Mountain Brigade would follow his commands.] After a detailed examination of the Target List for Neutralization In the City of Tehran (machine gun factory, Ministry of Post and Telegraph, Office of the Chief of Staff, etc.), SIS stated that the targets we had listed for neutralization were the correct ones and that we had assigned duties for components of the Third Mountain Brigade about as well as any other way they might suggest.

We next turned to an examination of our second military plan based upon the assumption that Carroll might be able to develop assets in Tehran capable of controlling three brigades. We all agreed that it would be extremely hazardous to base all of our hopes upon one brigade out of the five in Tehran and that, if possible, we should attempt to develop additional forces. SIS approved this plan and they then passed both plans up to a brigadier who returned them the next day without comment. During these discussions a cable arrived in London via Cyprus from Tehran in which Tehran Station reported General Zahedi's "military assets." This message confirmed all of our fears. For some time the Station had been attempting to persuade General Zahedi to list his military assets and to indicate how he hoped to use them.

At last General Zahedi reported. He claimed none of the five brigades in Tehran. His military plan assumed that he might be able to use the Imperial Guard, some troops from the Department of Army Transport, components from the Department of Police, and components of the Armed Customs Guard. He also hoped that Colonel [Timur Bakhtiar] might be able to bring troops to Tehran from [Kermanshah.] SIS asked Carroll to write for them an appreciation of Zahedi's plan. In that appraisal it was stated that he did not believe the Shah would sign a *farman* dismissing Mossadeq until Zahedi could indicate to him how Chief of Staff Riahi's control over the Tehran garrison could be broken; further, he felt that if Ajax were to succeed military assets must be developed within the five brigades in Tehran.

SIS agreed in London that military tasks should take the following priority:

1. Seizure and occupation of designated points.
2. Execution of arrest and detention lists.
3. Neutralization of pro-Mossadeq military forces in Tehran.
4. Neutralization of the city of Tehran.
5. Reinforcement of pro-Zahedi forces in Tehran by forces outside of the city.

These priorities were laid down because it was desired that communications be knocked out as soon as possible in order to prevent pro-Mossadeq forces and personnel from communicating with each other.

Carroll left London on the first available aircraft following these conferences, arrived in Tehran on 21 July, and got in touch with [Farzanegan.]

Sifting through [Farzanegan's] operational contact reports covering all of his important conversations in Tehran [after his arrival from the United States], two officers were noted as being of special promise. These were contact reports of conversations with Major General [Nadr Batmangelich] and with Colonel [Hassan Akhavi], both of whom were old and good friends of [Farzanegan]. These two officers reflected the fear of the Tudeh party that was becoming general after the Tudeh showing of 21 July. Goiran, Goodwin, and Carroll agreed that it was imperative that Carroll meet as soon as possible with an officer appointed by Zahedi to work on our military scheme. Zahedi never did designate a military secretariat, and it was necessary for us to develop our own. Because of General Zahedi's manifestly weak position among the military then on active duty, and because it became apparent that it would be necessary for CIA to seize the initiative and to furnish him with a military plan and military forces, the development of Colonel [Akhavi] was stepped up. [Farzanegan] was directed to determine what assets Colonel [Akhavi] might be able to lead us to. Colonel [Akhavi] first offered a "Plan A" which called for a military coup d'etat without explaining how it was to be accomplished. Then [Farzanegan] was pressed to persuade Colonel [Akhavi] to be more realistic, and on 30 July he received from Colonel [Akhavi] a plan which was more specific but still pitifully inadequate. Colonel [Akhavi] said he would execute arrests and target lists, neutralize military installations and non-cooperating forces within two hours; this was nonsense.

The most important thing Colonel [Akhavi] reported was that he was in touch with three young colonels who might possess important strength within the Tehran garrison. Colonel [Akhavi] also told [Farzanegan] that General [Batmangelich] lacked courage but would stiffen his back should the Shah appoint him Chief of Staff. Colonel [Akhavi] did not mention General Zahedi and did not seem to be in touch with him. [Farzanegan] told Colonel Akhavi that he could put Colonel [Akhavi] in touch with one or two Americans whom he had met in the United States.

At this time the Shah also indicated that he did not have control of important military assets.

Carroll met [Akhavi] and [Farzanegan] on 2 and 3 August and began staff planning. Colonel [Akhavi] was full of desire to do something, but had no idea of how to go about it. He said that he had friends who could control the Second and Third Mountain Brigades but did not trust either Colonel [Ashrafi], Commanding Officer of the Third Mountain Brigade [and an alleged SIS asset], or Colonel Momtaz, Commanding Officer of the Second Mountain

Brigade. Colonel [Akhavi] reported that General [Batmangelich] had told him the day before that if the Shah acted he was ready to perform any service whatsoever and to die for the Shah if necessary.

After these early meetings with Colonel [Akhavi], it became apparent that he, himself, was not in a position to command anything and was only hoping that he might persuade his friends to do so.

Carroll then met directly with Colonel [Akhavi] and his friend. The latter turned out to be Colonel [Zand-Karimi], [Colonel Komtaz's deputy]. Colonel [Zand-Karimi] reported a long list of assets within the Tehran garrison, principally among deputy commanders of brigades and regimental commanders. On 6, 7, and 8 August, Colonels [Akhavi, Zand-Karimi, Farzanegan], and Mr. Carroll carried on staff planning based upon the units commanded by friends whom [Zand-Karimi] claimed. Colonel [Zand-Karimi] stated that his primary friends were [Colonel Hamidi], of the Tehran police; [Colonel Ordubadi], of the Tehran Gendarmerie District; and [Colonel Mansurpur, Commanding Officer Iranian Cavalry]. He felt certain that ultimate victory would be ours through these friends, and through his friends who were regimental and battalion commanders, among these were important unit commanders in the Tehran garrison: [Colonel Rohani, Deputy Commander of the Third Mountain Brigade; Lt. Colonel Khosro-Panah, Commanding Officer of the Second Mountain Brigade Infantry Regiment; Lt. Colonel Yusefi, who was soon to be named Commanding Officer of the Third Mountain Brigade's Infantry Regiment.] Through these officers Colonel [Zand-Karimi] was in touch with every infantry battalion commander in Tehran and with most of the company commanders; however, those officers had not been formed into an organization and were not ready to overthrow Chief of Staff General Riahi's firm control of the Tehran garrison which he exercised through the Brigade Commanders in Tehran. For instance, if we were to succeed we must arrest Colonel Sharokh, Commanding Officer First Armored Brigade; Colonel Parsa, Commanding Officer First Mountain Brigade; and probably

Colonel Ashrafi, Military Governor and Commanding Officer of the Third Mountain Brigade. Colonel Novzari, Commanding Officer of the Second Armore Brigade would probably remain neutral but we felt it imperative that his deputy, Lt. Colonel Bahrami, be arrested.

It therefore became clear from the military point of view that success might depend upon whether or not General Riahi succeeded in arresting our friends before we arrested his, and that the test of strength would very largely rest upon the amount of security we were able to maintain while attempting to knit all of our friends into a functioning team.

It also was clear that we had to devise a scheme capable of carrying our operations in the event our first platoon of young officers was arrested. Carroll therefore worked for two nights with Colonels [Farzanegan and Zand-Karimi] devising a system which would work in the event our first team was arrested. The danger signal we adopted to alert battalion and company commanders to take independent action was the arrest of Colonel [Zand-Karimi] and of his closest friends. The weakness in our plan lay in the fact that the station would not be in a position to contact battalion and company commanders but would have to depend upon Colonel [Zand-Karimi] to do the job. While discussing this subject, Colonel [Zand-Karimi] stated that he would be able to contact lower unit commanders within 48 hours after receipt of the Shah's *farman*.

The hesitation of the Shah in signing the *farman* worked to our advantage for it gave us several more important days in which to discuss with Colonel [Zand-Karimi] the development of our final staff plans which was based upon the use of the units which his friends commanded. This problem was complicated by the fact that Colonel [Akhavi] became violently ill and was later forced to retire to his bed. As the climax approached, tension increased and it is not inconceivable that tension caused by fear had something to do with Colonel [Akhavi's] illness. Colonel [Akhavi] did remain on his feet long enough to speak to the Shah on 9 August in an interview which later proved vital to the success of the military phase of Ajax. Until Colonel [Akhavi] saw the Shah, he was not certain that our friends in the Tehran garrison would act without the Shah's approval. However, after talking with the Shah, Colonel [Akhavi] was able to tell Colonel [Zand-Karimi] that the Shah did desire military support in the event he should decide to sign the *farman*.

Colonel [Akhavi] was asked by the Shah whether or not the Army would back a *farman* dismissing Mossadeq. Colonel [Akhavi] told the Shah that he had been meeting with Carroll and that a reasonable staff plan was being prepared, one that assured victory if it were carried out properly. The Shah then asked [Akhavi] for the names of the officers who would cooperate, and Colonel [Akhavi] reported the same names which we had earlier submitted to the Shah through Asadollah Rashidian. He asked [Akhavi] to meet General Zahedi.

In reporting the substance of his audience with the Shah, Colonel [Akhavi] asked the station if the United States would support General Zahedi. He was told that it would.

Colonel [Zand-Karimi] also accepted General Zahedi. Both officers stated that they had not been in touch with General Zahedi for several months but believed him to be a very good leader.

During the nights of 11, 12 and 13 August, staff planning continued based upon the use of forty line commanders within the Tehran garrison. Colonel [Akhavi] met General Zahedi who agreed that General [Batmangelich] might be chief of staff. General [Batmangelich] expressed the desire to meet Carroll and to discuss plans with him, Farzanegan, Colonel [Akhavi], and Colonel [Zand-Karimi]. This meeting was postponed until we felt our staff plan was complete enough for General [Batmangelich] to act upon it. On 11 August Zahedi asked [Akhavi] to have [Farzanegan] come to see him. General Zahedi and [Farzanegan] talked for three hours. [Farzanegan] reported that General Zahedi was extremely appreciative of American assistance and asked [Farzanegan] to act as liaison officer between him-self and the Americans for military purposes; he also asked him to become his officer in charge of the Military Bureau which had been meeting with Carroll during the last week.

On 12 August Farzanegan took General [Batmangelich] to see

Zahedi, and General [Bamangelich] pledged General Zahedi all assistance. [Farzanegan] also took Colonel [Zand-Karimi] to see Zahedi and the latter reported to General Zahedi progress of military staff planning. In retrospect it would appear that under more favorable conditions we should have spent more time going over the staff plan with Zahedi and General [Batmangelich], for it was at this moment that the military phase of Ajax passed into Zahedi's hands, although Zahedi did not know any of the young officers involved and General [Batmangelich] knew only a few of them. During the afternoon of 15 August, Carroll met with General [Batmangelich] and the Military Secretariat composed of [Farzanegan,] Colonel [Akhavi,] and Colonel [Zand-Karimi]. The *farmans* were expected momentarily and much of the conversation revolved around the question of how long it would take Colonel [Zand-Karimi] to contact our friendly forty line commanders. After a long discussion everyone agreed action should commence within 48 hours of the receipt of the *farmans*. It was also agreed that Colonel [Nasiri, Commanding Officer of the Imperial Guard], would deliver the *farmans* to Mossadeq after he had sent the station a radio set attuned to Colonel [Zand-Karimi's] command net.

Colonel [Nasiri] flew to Ramsar with the unsigned *farmans* on 13 August.

HERE, SHAH REZA PAHLAVI in full military regalia. The Shah ruled Iran with an iron fist, surpassing any Iranian regime before or after in brutality and torture. For being placed in power, the Shah agreed to do what former Prime Minister Mossadeq never would: make foreign and domestic Iranian policy revolve around the best interests of the United States and Britain.

APPENDIX E

Military Critique Lessons
Learned from Ajax
Re Military Planning
Aspects of Coup d'Etat

I. The problem of Personnel Assessment

A. If CIA desires to overthrow a hostile government by employing armed forces against that government, then CIA must identify friendly forces, make contact with them, and successfully employ them.

B. The decision to attempt a military coup d'etat should only be made after it has been determined that potentially useful forces do exist. Distinction must be made in making this estimate of the situation between "grousers" and "activists." When attempting to estimate potential assets, experience has shown that it is vital to have as detailed biographical information as possible on all military personnel whose presence might bear upon the problem, including possible enemies as well as friends.

C. Biographical information cannot be collected in a short period of time. It must be reported on a basis of continuity and must include everything known about individual officers, no matter how trivial. Military attaches are the normal channels for these reports but Military Advisory Assistance Groups, where present, are the best source of this type of information because they work and take recreation side by side with indigenous officers. It has been our experience that too little emphasis is being placed upon this requirement; too often the files of officers contain only short references to an officer's assignments, promotions, decorations, omitting all personalia which could indicate who an officer really is, what makes him tick, who his friends are, etc.

D. Biographical files on CIA agents in armed forces are more complete but often these agents are found in G-2 sections and other staffs, and not among troop commanders.

E. Assuming that sufficient biographical information exists concerning military personnel and their motivations, our next task is to assess the character of each military person under review. The assessment of officers should be done with a clear appreciation of the traditions of the indigenous service in mind. For instance, the army in Iran has a modern tradition of defeat. The Iranian officer is usually indecisive and covers his inferiority with bombast and chest beating. Therefore the location of leaders who are willing to lead and to die is a hazardous occupation. Perhaps the Shah is a good example of the "typical" Iranian officer; his weaknesses are reflected throughout his Officer Corps. On the other hand, a true leader in the Army is worth his weight in gold for he truly will count for far more in Iran than in other countries where valor is traditional.

F. After personal assessment of officers has been completed, CIA will find good and bad officers within all factions or groups. Here political and patriotic motivations must be assessed as well as possible. The political milieu will underlay assessment of officers, and non-military operations might have to be prevailed upon to create conditions capable of intensifying or weakening motivations in such a way as to create potential assets which at the time of assessments do not yet exist.

G. Friendship toward "the free world," "the United States," "the United Nations," "white colonialism," and many other political motivations will be found in all countries. In Iran CIA found that officers were generally "pro-Shah," "pro-Mossadeq," or "fence sitters." The intensity of individual political motivations was different in each case, and was often less important than personal motivations such as ambition, jealousy, young officers' resentments of old officers and vice versa. There is no tradition of military revolutions, but Reza Shah did seize control of the government by using a military position as the springboard. Hence, the political motivation of officers and personal motivations within the political milieu have been and are factors to be considered in assessment of military personnel.

H. Of equal importance in Iran was the assessment of the Commander-in-Chief, the Shah, who also is the head of State. From the military point of view, assessment had to be made of the Shah as Commander-in-Chief, including his depth of influence, command ability, and courage under fire. His use as a focal point or fusing point around which military persons and groups might rally also had to be assessed.

Without stating reasons, our assessment of his usefulness was positive in these fields:

1. Head of State to dismiss hostile government.
2. Commander-in-Chief as rallying symbol.

Our assessment of these fields:

1. Commander-in-Chief as planner and participant in military action.

I. Turning from our assessment of the Shah, we concluded that the Shah as a symbol could be used to incite action on the part of important military personnel.

J. Our assessments of individual military persons led us to the conclusion that Major General Zahedi was the best suited officer available to lead forces for the Shah against the hostile government for these reasons:

1. He was the only man in Iran openly bidding for the prime ministership.

2. He thus displayed unique courage in that action.

3. He had displayed courage in the past, for as a soldier of 25 years he had been made a Brigadier General in recognition of combat leadership against the Bolsheviki.

4. His life had been saved by an American doctor after four of Zahedi's ribs had been removed.

5. He was known to be pro-American and had permitted his son, Ardeshir, to study in the United States for six years. He was a senior Major General and had won the respect of many senior and junior officers.

G. His negative qualifications were as follows:

a. He had been out of the army for several years and did not know young junior officers.

b. He was identified in some quarters as venal. His capacity for leading a coup d'etat was unknown; he had never distinguished himself as a staff officer, but primarily as a commander.

c. Most of his friends were drawn from among the civilian population—few were Army officers.

L. Specific assessment of line commanders in the Tehran garrison could not go forward in Washington until intelligence directives had been laid upon the field station. For instance, Headquarters did not know the names of any of the Brigade Commanders in Tehran, and to our surprise, neither did the G-2 Section, Pentagon [U.S. Army intelligence]; Headquarters did not possess any idea of the order of battle in Iran nor did G-2, Pentagon. Before specific assessment of line commanders could be made, therefore, Tehran Station had to report to Headquarters military information which should have been collected by military attaches on a day-to-day basis.

M. While assessment of individual officers was being made in Headquarters, the actual decisions had been taken by the Department of State to do everything possible to turn out Mossadeq. This decision to proceed found us with no clear picture of the military situation in Iran, without even a list of officers and their assignments, and with no operational assets among those officers in command positions. It must be understood, therefore, that swifter movement was required in all phases of our military actions to such an extent that assessments were made and decisions taken on a much less secure basis than would otherwise have been the case.

N. Our assessment of Mossadeq's Chief of Staff, Brigadier General Taghi Riahi, was done with care. We studied him in the light of his total personal environment, including a study of the persons with whom he lived, the persons he had removed from office, the persons he appointed to office, persons he had gathered in his staff, the political persons with whom he associated. From the political point of view, there was no doubt that Mossadeq had chosen his chief of staff very well. (We felt certain that Riahi would follow Mossadeq in a showdown, and not the Shah.) But from the military point of view, Brigadier General Riahi had several weaknesses. We could not be sure, but we had good ground to hope that Riahi's lack of command and combat experience would prove important if a test of military strength could be brought about. We did not question his personal courage and integrity. We found that he was residing with three of the outstanding members of the pro-Mossadeq Iranian Party and that he actually had led a pro-Mossadeq faction within the Army. He and most of his staff had been French-trained and were very thorough in staff work and very green in the field.

O. As the field began to report personalia concerning brigadier commanders in Tehran and in other parts of Iran, we were able to assess the situation with much greater clarity. It became evident that it would be necessary to arrest or remove most of the brigade commanders and to develop operational assets, for the most part, beneath that echelon of command. This assessment later proved to be correct and saved us much time and kept us from harm— from the security point of view. Because of the all-pervading necessity of drum-tight security, we could see from the beginning the necessity for approaching and developing only those persons with whom we stood a very good chance of success.

P. From all the above it can readily be seen that the possession of all-inclusive biographical information is vital to the success of any operation which includes large-scale use of military personnel. Failure can easily depend upon a mistake in the assessment of one officer and victory hinged upon it.

II. A. Military Intelligence as a basis for Action Intended to Overthrow Hostile Governments.

1. A war map should be kept by paramilitary officers in each station where revolutionary action may be required. Maps should be assembled of every scale of possible use. The complete order of battle should be posted on a current basis. The supply station as regards ammunition, gasoline and petrol, clothing and equipment, etc., must be watched very carefully. There may be no use sending a brigade into action against a hostile government when that brigade possesses only six rounds of ammunition per man.

2. Defensive measures taken by hostile governments should be watched very carefully. In Iran, Mossadeq's government assembled most of the motor transport into one motor pool; his government permitted only enough petrol for tanks to permit them to operate for one hour; the issuance of ammunition was reduced to an absolute minimum; and ammunition supply dumps were heavily reinforced (guarded). The signal code for the Iranian Army was changed only three weeks prior to the Mossadeq overthrow.

[REDACTED]

At two critical moments, Chief of Staff General Riahi assembled all officers in the Tehran garrison and made emotional appeals to their patriotism, equated by him with support for Mossadeq. List of officer's license plates on vehicles were called for by General Riahi, and in some cases officers were followed. Also, spot telephone checks were made to officers' homes in attempt to learn which officers were spending their evenings away from home.

B. It is also necessary to study all military installations which must be seized or protected. For that purpose it is necessary to have detailed drawings of important headquarters, of important communication centers, etc. In the beginning of Ajax we possessed none of this information, except for a few excellent sabotage studies made of civilian installations.

C. In an action of this sort it must be appreciated well in advance that key personnel and civilian installations must be seized. It should be possible to call upon many sources of information for assessment of political figures, but the collection of information concerning physical characteristics of telephone offices, radio stations, airports, etc., is a matter that can greatly be assisted when collected under the guidance of a paramilitary officer who understands what he is looking for; that is not to say that an excellent intelligence officer could not do the same but his intelligence directives should be carefully drawn.

D. Weather conditions may be absolutely vital to success and should be noted at least well in advance. Should fog exist, for instance, time and distance factors in staff planning may be thrown off entirely. Rain and storms might do the same. The question of whether or not to begin action by daylight or at night is a vital decision, and it must be made on the ground. In places where curfews exist, conditions may be radically altered by that fact. In other locations the habits of the people may be of extremely important military significance; for instance, the siesta habit, including the closing of most of the shops in business areas, may be important. Also, the day in the week observed as the religious day should be studied for possible usefulness as well as important holidays. Days which neutralize or tend to neutralize opposition groups should be studied with care; for instance, training of military units in some locations is rotated and it might be found that a hostile unit will be sent out of the area of action on a day upon which it may be possible to act.

E. Military information concerning G-1 sections [military intelligence] may prove extremely useful. In some cases it is possible to arrange for the replacement or reassignment of officers who are in the wrong position from our point of view. The placing of the right man in the right spot at the right time is of course the most important factor in all military operations and should under no circumstances be overlooked in operations of this kind.

F. Actions which might be taken against you should be studied very carefully and you should receive well in advance notice of measures of this kind before they are actually effected. It will also be understood that G-2 sections may possibly be used in places where panic may result in the hostile camp. In Iran we were greatly assisted by the fact that many groups of officers were suspected of planning a coup. As tension increased, reports of this sort also increased. Although they served to alert the hostile government, they also served to smokescreen our activities and the activities of our friends. This whole matter is naturally a matter of study under local conditions, but our experience may be of some assistance in places where similar circumstances exist.

G. It may also be entirely possible that other military groups are being forced to combat the hostile government, and in that case we should know who they are and what they intend to do. It may be necessary to split some of these groups, or it may be necessary to fuse them with our forces. In both cases our action must be delicately taken on the basis of very good information. Provocation must be carefully watched for, and remedial steps planned for and taken in the event any of our friends nibbles at the bait.

H. Information concerning our own friends is perhaps the most important field for collection. The appraisal of our own security situation on a continuous basis is a paramount consideration for current decision-making. In Iran we developed and recruited young colonels after very quick assessment, fully understanding the risk we were taking; at the same time, we attempted to probe and to delve in an effort to find out as much about our new recruits as possible.

I. If it is at all possible to develop secretly assets which can check up on the actions of our friends, it will be found extremely useful to have them, for it will be found that the military situation can become extremely fluid and it is absolutely vital to know who has been wounded, arrested, doubled, etc. Early warning of a security break should be provided for and a warning then established capable of reaching and warning other assets. This is particularly true during action phases.

J. Security controls may change from day to day and we should have information concerning the entire field. For instance, in the middle of an extremely fluid military situation it was necessary for one of our officers and for one of our principal agents to make hasty trips after curfew hours to cities eight and ten hours away from the capital. We were able to provide them with forged documents which proved absolutely necessary to the success of their missions.

K. Information concerning the available radio and telegraphic nets is extremely important. In Iran there is an Air Force radio net, gendarmerie radio net, Army radio net, railroad net, and an oil company telegraphic net. The number and extent of telegraphic nets is often surprising in any country and they must be studied very carefully for obvious reasons. At one stage in operation Project Ajax we used the overt governmental telegraphic system, using simple phrases for operational meaning (over-writing). Telephone systems are easy means for both hostile and friendly forces to communicate with each other, and information should be gathered on the extent to which central tapping services exist and, if possible, targets under tap should be identified. In Iran it was known that the Tudeh Party had penetrated the governmental communication system and, despite that fact, we relied upon that system because at one point all other means of communication broke down. The insecurity of that practice was realized but had to be accepted under the circumstances. In the signal center in the office of the chief of staff, or the signal center used by the Army Chief of Staff, is the single most important communication base available to a hostile opposition. If this center cannot be penetrated it should be neutralized and alternate means of communications established for friendly forces.

L. Information gathering can sometimes be of use during occasions in which it is necessary to fabricate "excuses for action."

Good penetrations of the hostile government might possibly turn up actions taken by the hostile government which have not been revealed to the public. In attempting to recruit personnel to your cause, it will always be necessary to provoke them to action when their motivation is insufficient to cause them to act under their own steam.

III. Military Planning as a Basis of Coup d'Etat

• The science of military planning is too deep and well known to be covered in this paper. Needless to say, those officers who are responsible for military planning should have had qualified experience in the armed forces in preparation for this assignment.

• In addition to a background in military planning, officers should also be experienced in clandestine operations. The basis of a coup d'etat is security which permits us to exercise operational surprise. The basis of security is good operational tradecraft which can only come from experience.

• It may be assumed that a military bureau composed of indigenous officers will be available for specific local planning, either from within the target country or from without. This military bureau can operate only when it possesses current and complete military intelligence.

• The military bureau may be designated by the leader-to-be of the new friendly government or may be composed independently of the leader-designee. In either case, clandestine tradecraft is a vital necessity.

• Whether or not a CIA officer shall be exposed to this military bureau will depend upon the local situation. In Iran we found it necessary to commit the CIA planner, who later found it necessary to participate in the operation itself on an equal basis with indigenous officers. It is obvious that this practice is an additional security risk which should be avoided if possible.

• Political arrest lists should be furnished to the CIA military planner, and it is his job to designate forces to execute such lists. Military and civilian targets for neutralizing and seizure by friendly forces should be drawn up by the CIA military officer and the military bureau.

• If possible, a CIA radio net should be created specifically for the coup d'etat tying our CIA field officer with the military bureau which in turn should be tied in to the headquarters and command units for friendly forces. Where this practice is not feasible, other means of communication should primarily be relied upon. But in all situations a primary and alternate means of communication among these elements should be created.

• Military planning should be based upon the principle that some elements [within] friendly forces will be exposed, and that our operation must not collapse on that account. Therefore, danger signals should be included which automatically call for movement from one phase to the other depending upon who or what units have been exposed to the hostile government. In Iran there was good reason to believe that danger signals so noted prior to the change of government were instrumental in keeping alive an operation which, to an outsider, appeared to have failed.

• The possibility of civil war must be accepted by our military planners and measures taken within the plan for the eventuality. Such an eventuality might possibly include the necessity for establishing a safebase for the new friendly government. Possibilities and eventualities stemming from civil war can only be seen upon the analysis of each local situation, but they are not difficult to foresee and should certainly be planned for.

• The creation of safehouse bases for operational contacts must be planned for and executed well in advance of the commitment of our friendly forces. Several safehouses or safebases should be found in order to maintain contact with friendly elements in the event one or more of our safehouses are blown. In cases where CIA personnel are all stationed within an embassy the operational situation demands that safehouses and safebases be established. These safehouses should ideally include radio, independent telephone, or other means of communications, depending upon the local situation. In situations in which it is necessary to cache money, ammunition, arms, clothing, food, and documents, safehouses should be found with secure keepers capable of securing these items.

• Support items such as automobiles, taxicabs, and other vehicles should be procured and kept sterile well in advance of the operational situation.

• Compartmentation of persons and units who compose our friendly forces should be made wherever possible. In the event a part of our operation be exposed, it is vital that interrogation not disclose our entire assets.

• Members of the military bureau should under no circumstances actively participate in the operation because under interrogation they would be in a position to disclose too much.

N. The military board should include both staff officers and line officers, and as many functional specialists as may be necessary under local conditions. A communications staff officer will be found very useful.

• Possibilities of blowback against the United States should always be in the back of the minds of CIA officers involved in this type of operation. Few, if any, operations are as explosive as this type. This fact makes it imperative that the best trained and experienced officers who can be found be assigned.

• Military planning should include the possibilities of complete failure and, therefore, should include an evacuation scheme for CIA and indigenous personnel who might be exposed. Aircraft of American military attaches, evasion and escape nets, and other operational assets might have to be employed. If none of these assets exists then hiding places should be created in advance of the operation which are kept sterile throughout.

• Commitments to friendly persons should be kept well within our ability to make good. In Iran we did not rely upon bribery because we felt that those officers who would accept bribes would probably betray the operation in the event of extreme difficulty, i.e., torture. In Iran we did not spend one cent in the purchase of officers.

• Forethought should also be given to the problem of care and keeping of wives and families of friendly officers.

• The possibility of using weapons of foreign-make should be kept well in mind in cases where American arms are not indigenous to the local area.

[REDACTED]

way as to neutralize entire cities through the use of road blocks, strong points, traffic control, curfews, new documentation, etc.

• Needless to say, a complete roster of officer assignments in the new army should be drawn well in advance in order that there be no confusion.

• Wherever possible it is much better to use the local army supply system than it is to create a new clandestine one. It also follows that it is much better to conduct the operation from within the country than it is to attempt a cross-border operation. It is also much easier to execute the operation when CIA officers are present than it is when CIA officers are outside the country. Deep cover personnel should be used in order to prevent severe blow-back whenever it is possible to do so.

SUMMARY

BY THE END OF 1952, IT HAD BECOME CLEAR that the Mossadeq government in Iran was incapable of reaching an oil settlement with interested Western countries was reaching a dangerous and advanced stage of illegal deficit financing; was disregarding the Iranian constitution in prolonging Premier Mohammed Mossadeq's tenure of office; was motivated mainly by Mossadeq's desire for personal power; was governed by irresponsible policies based on emotion; had weakened the Shah and the Iranian Army to a dangerous degree; and had cooperated closely with the Tudeh (Communist) Party of Iran. In view of these factors, it was estimated that Iran was in real danger of falling behind the Iron Curtain; if that happened it would mean a victory for the Soviets in the Cold War and a major setback for the West in the Middle East. No remedial action other than the covert action plan set forth could be found to improve the existing state of affairs.

It was the aim of the Ajax project to cause the fall of the Mossadeq government; to reestablish the prestige and power of the Shah; and to replace the Mossadeq government with one which would govern Iran according to constructive policies. Specifically, the aim was to bring to power a government which would reach an equitable oil settlement, enabling Iran to become economically sound and financially solvent, and which would vigorously prosecute the dangerously strong Communist Party.

Once it had been determined definitely that it was not in American interests for the Mossadeq government to remain in power and CIA had been so informed by the Secretary of State in Karch 1953, CIA began drafting a plan whereby the aims stated above could be realized through covert action. An estimate entitled "Factors Involved in the Overthrow of Mossadeq" was completed on 16 April 1953. It was here determined that an overthrow of Mossadeq was possible through covert operations. In April it was determined that CIA should conduct the envisioned operation jointly with the British Secret Intelligence Service (SIS). By the end of April, it was decided that CIA and SIS officers would draw up a plan on Cyprus which would be submitted to CIA and SIS Headquarters, and to the Department of State and the Foreign Office for final approval. On 3 June 1953, U.S. Ambassador Loy Wesley Henderson arrived in the United States where he was fully consulted with regard to the objective and aims, as stated above, as well as CIA's intentions to design covert means of achieving the objective and aims.

The plan was completed by 10 June 1953 at which time Mr. Kermit Roosevelt, Chief of the Near East and Africa Division, CIA (who carried with him the views of the Department of State, CIA, and Ambassador Henderson); Mr. Roger Goiran, CIA Chief of Station, Iran; and two CIA planning officers met in Beirut to consider the plan. With minor changes the operational proposal was submitted to the SIS in London on 14 June 1953.

On 19 June 1953, the final operational plans agreed upon by Mr. Roosevelt for CIA and by British Intelligence in London, was submitted in Washington to the Department of State; to Mr. Allen W. Dulles, Director of CIA; and to Ambassador Henderson for approval. Simultaneously, it was submitted to the British Foreign Office by SIS for approval. The Department of State wanted to be assured of two things before it would grant approval of the plan:

1. that the United States Government could provide adequate grant aid to a successor Iranian government so that such a government could be sustained until an oil settlement was reached;

2. that the British government would signify in writing, to the satisfaction of the Department of State, its intention to reach an early oil settlement with a successor Iranian government in a spirit of good will and equity.

The Department of State satisfied itself on both of these scores.

In mid-July 1953, the Department of State and the British Foreign Office granted authorization for the implementation of the Ajax project, and the Director of CIA obtained the approval of the President of the United States. The SIS, with the concurrence of the CIA Director and Ambassador Henderson, proposed that Mr. Roosevelt assume field command in Tehran of the final phases of the operation. It was determined by the Department of State that it would be advisable for

Ambassador Henderson to postpone his return to Iran, from Washington consultation, until the operation had been concluded. Arrangements were made jointly with SIS whereby operational liaison would be conducted on Cyprus where a CIA officer would be temporarily stationed, and support liaison would be conducted in Washington. Rapid three-way communications were arranged through CIA facilities between Tehran, Cyprus, and Washington. The time set for the operation was mid-August.

In Iran, CIA and SIS propaganda assets were to conduct an increasingly intensified propaganda effort through the press, handbills, and the Tehran clergy in a campaign designed to weaken the Mossadeq government in any way possible. In the United States, high-ranking U.S. officials were to make official statements which would shatter any hopes held by Premier Mossadeq that America economic aid would be forthcoming, and disabuse the Iranian public of the Mossadeq myth that the United States supported his regime.

General Fazlollah Zahedi, former member of Mossadeq's cabinet, was chosen as the most suitable successor to the Premier since he stood out as the only person of stature who had consistently been openly in opposition to Mossadeq and who claimed any significant following. Zahedi was to be approached by CIA and be told of our operation and its aim of installing him as the new prime minister. He was to name a military secretariat with which CIA would conclude a detailed staff plan of action.

From the outset, the cooperation of the Shah was considered to be an essential part of the plan. His cooperation was necessary to assure the action required of the Tehran military garrisons, and to legalize the succession of a new prime minister. Since the Shah had shown himself to be a man of indecision, it was determined that pressure on him to cooperate would take the following forms:

1. The Shah's dynamic and forceful twin sister, Princess Ashraf Pahlavi, was to come from Europe to urge the Shah to dismiss Mossadeq. She would say she had been in contact with U.S. and UK officials who had requested her to do so.

2. Arrangements were made for a visit to Iran by General H. Norman Schwarzkopf, former head of the U.S. Gendarme Mission, whom the Shah liked and respected. Schwarzkopf was to explain the proposed project and get from the Shah signed farmans (royal decrees)

dismissing Mossadeq, appointing Zahedi, and calling on the army to remain loyal to the Crown.

3. The principal indigenous British agent, whose bona fides had been established with the Shah, was to reinforce Schwarzkopf's message and assure the Shah that this was a joint U.S.-UK action.

4. Failing results from the above, Mr. Roosevelt, representing the President of the United States, would urge the Shah to sign the above-mentioned farmans. When received, the farmans would be released by CIA to Zahedi on the day called for in the plan. On D-Day, the Shah was to be at some location outside of Tehran so that Zahedi, armed with the royal farmans and with military support, could take over the government without danger of the Shah's reversing his stand, and to avoid any attempt on the Shah's life.

Through agents in the Tehran military, CIA was to ensure, to the degree possible, Tehran army cooperation in support of the Shah-appointed new prime minister.

The following public statements made in the United States had tremendous impact on Iran and Mossadeq, and contributed greatly to Mossadeq's downfall:

1. The publication, on 9 July 1953, of President Eisenhower's 29 June 1953 letter to Premier Mossadeq made it clear that increased aid would not be forthcoming to Iran.

2. The Secretary of State's press conference of 28 July 1953 stated that ". . . . The growing activities of the illegal Communist Party in Iran and the toleration of them by the Iranian government has caused our government concern. These developments make it more difficult to grant aid to Iran."

3. The President's Seattle speech at the Governors' convention, in which he stated that the United States would not sit by and see Asian countries fall behind the Iron Curtain, had definite effect.

In cooperation with the Department of State, CIA had several articles planted in major American newspapers and magazines which, when reproduced in Iran, had the desired psychological effect in Iran and contributed to the war of nerves against Mossadeq.

After considerable pressure from Princess Ashraf and General Schwarzkopf, and after several meetings with Mr. Roosevelt, the Shah finally signed the required farmans on 15 August 1953. Action was set for 16 August. However, owing to a security leak in the Iranian military, the chief of the Shah's bodyguards assigned to seize Mossadeq with the help of two truckloads of pro-Shah soldiers, was overwhelmed by superior armed forces still loyal to Mossadeq. The balance of the military plan was thus frustrated for that day. Upon hearing that the plan had misfired, the Shah flew to Baghdad. This was an act of prudence and had been at least partially foreseen in the plan. Zahedi remained in hiding in CIA custody. With his key officers, he eluded Mossadeq's security forces which were seeking to apprehend the major opposition elements.

Early in the afternoon of 17 August 1953, Ambassador Henderson returned to Tehran. General Zahedi, through a CIA-arranged secret press conference and through CIA covert printing facilities, announced to Iran that he was legally prime minister and that Mossadeq had staged an illegal coup against him. CIA agent assets disseminated a large quantity of photographs of the farmans, appointing Zahedi prime minister and dismissing Mossadeq. This had tremendous impact on the people of Tehran who had already been shocked and angered when they realized that the Shah had been forced to leave Iran because of Mossadeq's actions. U.S. Ambassador Burton Y. Berry, in Baghdad, contacted the Shah and stated that he had confidence that the Shah would return soon to Iran despite the apparent adverse situation at that time. Contact was also established with the Shah in Rome after he had flown there from Baghdad. Mr. Roosevelt and the station consistently reported that Mossadeq's apparent victory was misleading; that there were very concrete signs that the army was still loyal to the Shah; and that a favorable reversal of the situation was possible. The station further urged both the British Foreign Office and the Department of State to make a maximum effort to persuade the Shah to make public statements encouraging the army and populace to reject Mossadeq and to accept Zahedi as prime minister.

On 19 August 1953, a pro-Shah demonstration, originating in the bazaar area, took on overwhelming proportions. The demonstration appeared to start partially spontaneously, revealing the fundamental prestige of the Shah and the public alarm at he undisguised republican move being started by the Communists as well as by certain National Frontists. Station political action assets also contributed to the beginnings of the pro-Shah demonstrations. The Army very soon joined the pro-Shah movement and by noon of that day it was clear that Tehran, as well as certain provincial areas, were controlled by pro-Shah street groups and army units. The situation was such that the above-mentioned military plan could then be implemented. At the station's signal, Zahedi came out of hiding to lead the movement. He first broadcast over Radio Tehran and announced that the government was his. The General Staff offices were then seized, Mossadeq's home was gutted, and pro-Mossadeq politicians and officers arrested. By the end of 19 August, the country was in the hands of the new Premier, Zahedi, and members of the Mossadeq government were either in hiding or were incarcerated.

The Shah returned shortly to Iran where he was given a rousing popular reception. The Shah was deeply moved by the fact that his people and army had revolted in the face of adversity against a vindictive Mossadeq and a Communist Party riding the crest of temporary victory and clearly planning to declare Iran a republic. The Shah felt for the first time that he had the mandate of his people, and he returned determined to regain firm control of the army.

In order to give Zahedi badly needed immediate financial assistance so that month-end payrolls could be met before the United States could provide large scale grant aid, CIA covertly made available $5,000,000 within two days of Zahedi's assumption of power.

INDEX

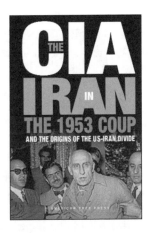

More Great Books from AFP . . .

Call 1-888-699-NEWS to order or see form in back

BRAINWASHED FOR WAR: Programmed to Kill

In *Brainwashed for War: Programmed to Kill*, written by internationally renowned Malaysian author Matthias Chang, we learn that we Americans have been brainwashed for war our entire lives. From the Cold War of our youths to Vietnam and now the so-called "War Against Terror" we have been lied to, mind-controlled and duped by president after president with the goal of making us mindless supporters of bloody war. And how many of the wars of the 20th (and now 21st) century have actually been necessary for the defense of the United States? Tracing back four decades and more, *Brainwashed for War* documents the atrocities carried out by the imperialist, Zionist-driven forces whose goal it is to subjugate the peoples of the world. Including 200 pages of detailed and highly-readable, eye-opening classified documents. Softcover, 556 pages, $30. No S&H.

Get *Brainwashed* and *Future FastForward* for just $50.

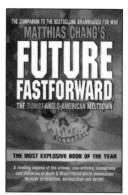

FUTURE FASTFORWARD: *The Zionist Anglo-American Empire Meltdown*

Is the alliance between the United States, the British Empire, and Israel a paper tiger or a mighty empire? Is global "Empire Capitalism" about to come crashing down? Will there be a worldwide "people's war" against the super-capitalists and their Zionist allies? Is nuclear war inevitable? These are just some of the provocative questions addressed in *Future FastForward*, a forthright, no-holds-barred new book by a prominent Asian political figure and globe-trotting diplomat. In *Future FastForward*, author Matthias Chang, former top-level political secretary for Malaysia's Dr. Mahathir Mohammad, takes a stark look at the realities of global power politics and the ultimate and inevitable consequences for the not-so-secret forces that are behind the push for a New World Order. The Power Elites of the Zionist Anglo-American Axis have been in control of the political systems throughout the world and, in all probability, there is not a single country in which their cunning and evil influence has not been felt. Softcover, 400 pages, $25. No S&H. SPECIAL COMBO—*Brainwashed for War* PLUS *Future FastForward* for just $50! You save $5.

THE HIGH PRIESTS OF WAR:
The Secret History of America's Neo-Cons

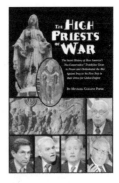

The High Priests of War tells the secret history of how America's neo-conservative Trotskyites came to power and orchestrated the war against Iraq as the first step in their drive for global power. This is the only full-length book on the "neo-cons" that tells the entire story—uncensored from start to finish. The book is now being circulated internationally and is being translated into a variety of languages, acclaimed as the one book that explains the "who, what, when, where, why and how" of the tragic involvement of the United States in the Iraq war. This fast-reading, carefully-documented 144-page volume has helped spread the word about the REAL reason for the Iraq war and how it is all part of a grand design that is being suppressed by the Controlled Media. Softcover, 144 pages, $19.95. No S&H.

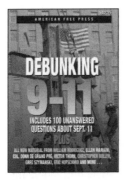

DEBUNKING 9-11:
100 Unanswered Questions About Sept. 11

All of AFP's best reporting on the Sept. 11 tragedies plus commentaries from survivors and researchers. In AFP's Debunking 9-11, you'll get never-before published commentaries from William Rodriguez, the Trade Center's "last man out," and Ellen Mariani, crusading wife of one of the victims killed on 9-11, renowned Pentagon insider Col. Donn de Grand Pré and many more PLUS all of AFP's groundbreaking coverage of the event from the beginning: the spies operating in New York; the many theories put forth by independent researchers who reject the government's explanation of many of the events of Sept. 11; alternative theories as to why the twin towers collapsed; detailed information from a dozen sources presenting evidence of foreknowledge by the government and foreign intelligence agencies of the event; scientific debate over what really happened at the Pentagon on Sept. 11 and theories as to the downing of Flight 93. Booklet, color cover, 108 pages, $19.95 for one. Bulk prices available. No S&H.

THE NEW JERUSALEM: Zionist Power in America

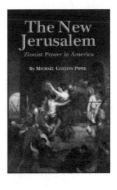

This explosive study combines in 184 pages all of the amazing facts and figures documenting the massive accumulation of wealth and power by those who have used that influence to direct the course of U.S. foreign and domestic policy today. While there are many historical books on "the Israeli lobby" and about Zionist intrigues, etc, this is the only book that brings things "up to date" and constitutes a bold and thorough inquiry. Softcover, 176 pages, $19.95. No S&H.

JIM TUCKER'S BILDERBERG DIARY

American Free Press reporter Jim Tucker has spent the last 25 years of his life tracking down a group of the world's richest and most influential industry magnates, bankers, media moguls and world leaders that meets every year in complete secrecy in some of the poshest venues the world has to offer. What's so amazing about this? The mainstream news media denies this group even exists! Only Jim Tucker—alone among American journalists—has been able to crack the code of silence surrounding the Bilderberg meetings. Only Jim Tucker has penetrated these meetings and reported on the nefarious goings on inside despite armed guards, attack dogs and barbed wire fences. Yes—Bilderberg does exist and YES their meetings are more than impromptu "tea and crumpet" parties as their apologists insist. And here is Jim's story—the result of a quarter decade of hard-nosed news reporting and hair-raising infiltration efforts. Softcover, 272 pages. No charge for S&H. Once copy is $25. No S&H.

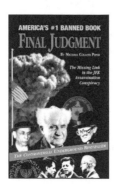

FINAL JUDGMENT: *The Missing Link in the JFK Assassination Conspiracy*

This massive 768-page volume is just now back from the printer in the second printing of its Sixth Edition, containing explosive new material. More than 45,000 copies of previous editions of this book are in circulation here and around the world, documenting—just as Israeli nuclear whistle-blower Mordechai Vanunu has said—that JFK's obstinate efforts to prevent Israel from building nuclear weapons of mass destruction played a critical role in the conspiracy behind JFK's assassination. On the strength of this amazing book, Piper has been invited all over the world to discuss his findings—everywhere from the Arab world to Moscow to Malaysia and Japan. Softcover, 768 pages, 1,000+ footnotes, $25. No charge for S&H.

DIRTY SECRETS:

Crime, Conspiracy & Cover-Up During the 20th Century
Here's an amazing collection of the writings (many never before seen in print), transcripts of uncensored interviews with Michael Collins Piper, reviews of his works and much more—all compiled in one "must-read" volume. Read where Piper's investigations have led him on such explosive topics as the King and JFK assassinations, the OKC bombing, the attack on the *USS Liberty*, the suppression of freedom of speech in America today, the power of the Zionist lobby and more. Compiled by Wing TV's Victor Thorn. Softcover, 256 pages. No charge for S&H. One copy is $22. No S&H.

American Free Press
Special Subscription Deal

There is no other paper in America like *American Free Press* (AFP). Every week the hard-driving journalists at *American Free Press* dig for the truth—no matter where the facts may lead. AFP's reporting has been lauded by prominent personalities across the globe, while here at home the controlled media and global power elite try their best to make you believe what you are getting in mainstream publications and on the nightly news is "the whole truth." Nothing could be further from reality!

From the unanswered questions about 9-11, the free trade fiasco, the happenings in our corrupt Congress, uncontrolled immigration, to alternative health news and more, AFP tackles the toughest issues of the day with a candid and provocative reporting style that has earned us a host of devoted followers—and powerful enemies.

Isn't it time you started getting a fresh, honest approach to the news that can make or break the future of you and your family?

You'll find all that in AFP plus lots more. AFP is guaranteed to provide all the "sizzle" we promise or we will refund the unused portion of your subscription—no questions asked!

Special "FREE BOOKS" Offer!

Get a FREE copy of Michael Collins Piper's *The High Priests of War: The Secret History of the Neo-Cons* ($19.95 retail) when you subscribe to AFP for ONE year (52 yearly issues). Get TWO FREE BOOKS—*The High Priests of War* PLUS *The New Jerusalem: Zionist Power in America*—when you subscribe to AFP for TWO years (104 issues) for $99. Send payment to AFP, 645 Pennsylvania Avenue SE, Suite 100, Washington, D.C. 20003 using the coupon in the back. Call AFP toll free at 1-888-699-NEWS (6397) to charge.